I0790452

BENT POLES,

HAPPY SOULS

Fishing Stories Gleaned from Sixty Years of Journaling

TOM FRIEDEMANN

Archway Publishing books may be ordered through booksellers or by contacting:

Archway Publishing
1663 Liberty Drive
Bloomington, IN 47403
www.archwaypublishing.com
844-669-3957

Scripture quotations taken from the (NASB®) New American Standard Bible®, Copyright © 1960, 1971, 1977, 1995, 2020 by The Lockman Foundation. Used by permission. All rights reserved. www.lockman.org

ISBN: 978-1-6657-2274-2 (sc)
ISBN: 978-1-6657-2276-6 (hc)
ISBN: 978-1-6657-2275-9 (e)

Library of Congress Control Number: 2022907873

Print information available on the last page.

Archway Publishing rev. date: 05/20/2022

For he will be like a tree planted by the water that extends its
roots by a stream, and will not fear when the heat comes: but
its leaves will be green, and it will not be anxious in a year of
drought, nor cease to yield fruit

—Jeremiah 17:8

CONTENTS

ACKNOWLEDGMENTS

I would like to express my appreciation to the following people for what they did to make this book possible.

Cindy Friedemann, my wife and frequent fishing partner who provided editing assistance and advice.

Alan (A. B.) Friedemann, my cousin and lifelong fishing companion who read every chapter as soon as I completed it and gave me feedback.

Jim Friedemann, my son and loyal fishing buddy since he was old enough to handle a rod. Jim provided the cover art from a painting he did at age twelve. Who would have thought back in 1980 that I would be using a painting he made as a boy over four decades ago for the cover of this book?

INTRODUCTION

Soon after I retired and moved to Edmond, Oklahoma, I learned about a small group of my old high school buddies from the class of '65 who were meeting every Friday at the local Mazzio's pizza restaurant in Stillwater, Oklahoma. Some of these guys I hadn't seen in over fifty years, and I was amazed at how old people my age looked, but it was good to catch up with everybody and talk about things that only a fellow Stillwater High School Pioneer could relate to. With all of us either retired or partially retired, one of our guys, Dr. Robert Breedlove, who had moved back to his hometown to practice dermatology, asked the question, If we had it to do all over again, would we choose the same career path? When it came to my turn, I responded without hesitation, "In a heartbeat." I wouldn't change a single thing about the decision I made to pursue a career in education, especially career-tech education. I can't think of anything more rewarding to do for my life's work than to wake up every morning knowing that what I am about to do that day is going to make a difference in someone's life. I mean, what's more rewarding than equipping a person with the skills he or she needs to be successful in the workplace?

For forty-nine years I woke up every day thinking I was helping solve Oklahoma's workforce shortage, one student at a time. One of the most rewarding days of my professional life came when Ken Koch, our director of marketing and communications at Francis Tuttle Technology Center, brought to my office a tweet from one of our automotive technician students. His tweet simply read, "Francis Tuttle is the only reason I keep wanting to go to school." For those of you who may not know how career-tech programs work in Oklahoma, we are an integral part of the public education system, specializing in providing technical education programs at both the secondary and postsecondary levels. We have our own district taxing base and elected board of education, and we operate independently from the comprehensive public school districts. Our postsecondary students pay tuition and can attend all day (six hours) while our high school students attend half days (three hours) tuition free as part of their public education in the state. High School juniors and seniors spend the other three hours of their school day attending their academic classes at a local comprehensive high school. So, in essence, what this young man was saying was that the only reason he was continuing with his academic education at his local high school was because of the opportunity it afforded him to enroll in his automotive technician class at Francis Tuttle for three hours every day.

I was so impressed by his open display of fondness on social media for our school that I visited his class that very next day to meet him personally. What a neat compliment he gave us through his unsolicited tweet! When I walked into the automotive shop and asked his instructor if I could speak with him, I could tell by the expression on his face that he thought the student was in big-time trouble for something. It's not often the superintendent pulls a student out of class to personally talk with him, so this just had to be a bad thing—or so he thought. I told the student how much I appreciated his tweet and that I just wanted to thank him for validating what we did at the school every day. He seemed a little shocked at first and replied, "Why wouldn't I love it here? At Francis

Tuttle I'm learning a skill that I can use the rest of my life to make a great living someday. And besides that, it's just fun to learn about working on cars."

I later had the student's tweet framed, and I proudly displayed it in my office. It also became part of my elevator speech to legislators and other leaders in our community. Of course, I complimented his instructor as well for doing such a good job of establishing in his students a passion for acquiring the necessary skills to be successful in their chosen field of work. That kind of passion is exactly what our employers are looking for in their workforce. It seems like every single day of my forty-nine-year career, I was blessed to hear of experiences like this in one form or another from either our students or from one of the many companies and businesses that employed them.

I can honestly say that my first day of work at age twenty-two as a teacher in Putnam City West High School in Oklahoma City was just as exciting as my last day of work at age seventy-one, as superintendent of the Francis Tuttle Technology Center. But once I made the decision to retire, I never looked back. Rather, I eagerly looked forward to my next challenge, and that was to refine my fly-fishing skills to the highest level possible and approach each new day fishing with as much excitement and passion as I did every day working in the field of career-tech education. I had lived the dream for forty-nine years, loving what I did for a living, and now it was time to continue that dream by spending more time on the water doing what I had first learned to love as a small boy growing up on a farm southeast of Stillwater, Oklahoma. Today I'm living a new dream one fish at a time. The dream comes to life every time the pole gets bent!

CHAPTER 1

ADJUSTING TO RETIREMENT

A few months after I had formally announced my retirement, I got some wonderful advice at a Rotary Club meeting from Jim Daniel, a local longtime banker. He said, "I heard you were retiring from Francis Tuttle."

I replied, "Yes. After putting on a starched shirt and tie for fifty-five years, it's going to be a little strange just waking up and not going to my closet with a purpose."

He said, "Tom, just always remember, it's not what you retire from but what you retire to that's really important."

That statement really got to me, as I had worried a great deal about how I was going to fill up my time every day beginning July 1. My identity for forty-nine years was as a teacher and administrator who had worked in that field all his adult life. What or who would I be after I retired? There wouldn't be anybody from my administrative staff asking me about what we should do with an instructional program that had suffered low enrollment or low job placement for the past two years. No legislator was going to call me on the phone and ask for my opinion on how a piece of legislation he or she was considering would impact career-tech education. There would be no graduation ceremonies to speak at, with hundreds of hands to shake as the graduates walked across the stage. There would be no school board meetings to prepare for. Just who would I be after June 30, 2019?

When you grow up on a farm as I did, you begin working as soon after you've fully mastered the skill to walk. My earliest memories of working are those of feeding over 250 chickens by spreading oats on the ground. I can remember pouring a gallon at a time on the ground in the pattern of my name and recalling how cool it was that the chickens were eating in a formation that spelled "Tommy." It was like watching the halftime performance from the top of the stadium as the marching band spelled out "OSU Cowboys." That was a powerful feeling for a young lad. Later, as soon as I was able to master the skill of not breaking eggs, I was in charge of going to the chicken house and gathering them into a bucket for eventual sale to the Stillwater Hatchery. Oh, how I hated that job because of the occasional painful pecks I'd receive from a laying hen who took great offense at me depriving her of a day's work. Or even worse was the fear of finding a snake that might be on the nest, grabbing a quick meal of fresh eggs.

As I got older, more chores were added to my responsibilities, which included milking cows, working the ground with the tractor, and helping with the annual wheat harvest. When I turned sixteen and could drive, I began working at a local department store and selling men's clothing as part of my responsibilities from being a student in my high school vocational distributive education class, which just happened to be taught by my father's brother, Uncle Gus. That's when I began dressing up every day for part-time work at C. R. Anthony's and then later at Katz Department Store in downtown Stillwater. Mom would spend a great deal of time washing and starching my shirts so I could present myself to the customer as somebody who knew a lot about clothing. Picking out the right tie was a skill I picked up myself with some help from the Wembley tie salesman who would call on our store.

So productive work was always an important part of growing up and becoming an adult, and I was a little apprehensive about this next step in my life called retirement. I had heard many stories of people becoming bored and even depressed by the prospect of not having anything productive to do all day and eventually reentering the workforce somewhere just to stay busy. Some of my buddies told me how they had flunked retirement, and I had witnessed them taking up everything from consulting work to greeting folks at the local big box discount store. But after being at the top of the food chain for the last decade, I just couldn't visualize myself doing anything similar.

About that same time, I always enjoyed reading articles in magazines about retired people who found a second career in something they were truly passionate about but had always been reluctant to pursue full-time for fear that they could never make a decent living at it. But with good, sound investing of their financial resources during their peak earning years, they were able to secure a comfortable enough retirement income that allowed them to finally engage in what they'd always really wanted to do. For me, that was fishing, and I had been doing it since I was a six-year-old and had even journaled my fishing trips since I was nine. So I thought I was pretty good at it and had the data to back it up.

TRIP NO. 3

Lake or River _Uncle Chuck pond_

Location _Perry Okla._

Date _May 30, 19__ Kind of Day _Warm_

Wind Direction _____ Lake Surface _____

Hours of Best Fishing _____

Best Fishing Depth _____ No. Fish Caught _2_

Kind of Fish Caught _Bass Channel Catfish_

Weight of Largest _4 4 oz. Cat._

Method Used _Set cork deep Waitted tell it went down_

Bait _Dead Minnow_

Rod _9 Weber_

Reel _____

Line _____

EXTRA NOTES

My first crude attempt to journal my fishing trips at age nine. Sixty-five years later, I'm still doing it.

Now, fishing as a career path is somewhat limited regarding what one can do. Figuring out how I could make it work was going to be a little bit tricky. You can fish commercially, though the options for that are significantly limited if you live in a land-locked state like Oklahoma. You can guide, but watching other people catch fish never had a lot of appeal to me. You can work in a bait and tackle shop, and while I gave that option some serious consideration, I had gotten my fill of retailing from the six years I worked part-time selling men's clothing at Katz and Anthony's as a high school and college student. Being confined to the four walls of any type of store just didn't seem to be a good fit for me. Tournament fishing wasn't really practical at my age, and the limited experience I had doing it when I owned a bass boat, too often left me empty in terms of achieving the joy that I had always cherished from the sport. And I certainly could never make a living selling my personally tied flies to a local fly shop. My ego simply could not endure the humiliation of the laughter that would surely come from the fly shop owner when he would be obliged to say, "You expect me to sell these to my customers?"

Then, with some encouragement from my wife, Cindy, and from Ed Godfrey, outdoor editor with the *Oklahoman* newspaper, I one day said to myself, "I think I'll write a book. That's what I'll retire to!" I retired June 30, 2019, and immediately began work on my book. I purchased a computer, carved out an office area in our new home in Edmond where I could overlook the lake for inspiration, and began going through my journals to see if there was anything interesting to write about. The biggest barrier that I had personally was imagining that anyone would be interested in reading about my experiences. That kind of changed when I enrolled in an evening class at Francis Tuttle titled The Joy of Writing. Some of our assignments in that class consisted of writing short stories about what we were passionate about and then reading them aloud to the class for a critique from our fellow classmates and instructor. To my surprise, it appeared that a lot of people in my class, most of whom didn't fish, actually enjoyed my writings, thereby giving me the confidence I needed to begin writing a book.

My first book was published on September 23, 2020, and was titled *If It Were Easy, They'd Call It Catchin'.* In the first quarter, it sold pretty well and had some very nice reviews from Amazon customers who also gave it an overall rating of 4.6 stars. As a result, I felt encouraged to write a second book and maybe officially refer to myself as "author" instead of "retired educator." Not that there's anything wrong with being an educator. I loved being a teacher and school administrator, but putting the word *retired* in front of any title, to me, just meant that I was no longer relevant in that field and had been officially turned out to pasture and waiting out my days for entrance through those pearly gates.

My old business cards used to say "Superintendent and CEO." My new business cards read "Author and Fly-Fishing Enthusiast." Now that I have my new title, I feel as though retirement is just another necessary step in my lifelong pursuit of who I am and what I can ultimately contribute to society as a living creature on this precious earth. Retirement has been a wonderful gift. I fish when I want to, write when I can't fish, and spend quality time with family and friends doing the types of things that make me happy.

CHAPTER 2

SIXTEEN "YOU REALLY SHOULDS"

I've always been intrigued by lists. That's partly how I managed to get three college degrees. As a student, I would make lists of answers to questions I thought might be on a test and then start the first word of each item on the list with a letter that created an acronym that was easy to remember. If I remembered the acronym, I could usually remember the items on the list. Lists are more likely to be remembered if they make sense and they help to organize desired behaviors. I make a to-do list every evening before I go to bed and keep it somewhere on my person during the following day as a constant reminder of what I need to accomplish so I feel as though I've had a productive day. I like to think that God knew about all this when on Mount Sinai He handed Moses two stone tablets that contained all the "thou shalt nots" and "thou shalts" that we need to go by as we live out our lives on Earth. It was the first list I can recall remembering by heart in Pastor Duis's confirmation class at Salem Lutheran Church in Stillwater, Oklahoma. It was the start to my list-making regime as a daily practice.

I've made a list for fishing that has been helpful to me throughout the years, but unlike the Ten Commandments, which contain both some thou shalts as well as some thou shalt nots, all of mine are strictly thou shalts (or, more politely stated, "you really shoulds). I call them the Sixteen You Really Shoulds:

Sixteen "You Really Shoulds"

1. **You really should dry your flies before putting them back in the fly box.** This is something I learned from my good friend Tom Adams on one of my first fly-fishing trips. He would always make sure the fly boxes he used during the day were left open in an area where they could receive plenty of fresh air so they could thoroughly dry out before the next day of fishing. I learned the hard way what the consequences were for not doing this. In my first year of being a fly-fisher, I was proud of the inventory of Woolly Buggers that I had accumulated. I learned early on what a productive pattern it was, and it became my first go-to fly. Then one day I opened a fly box after several weeks of not fishing and found nothing but loose feathers and a bunch of rusty hooks with chenille wrapped around them. They had all become terminally ill with a severe case of mildew or some type of feather rot. I was shocked and heartbroken, because many of them represented some great memories of fish caught, and now they were all dead to me. Of course, it also severely

limited my ability to catch fish that day. There are consequences for ignorance.

2. **You really should dry your fly line after each fishing trip.** I hear stories of how fly line needs to be replaced every few years or so. I personally think that's hogwash and is just a marketing gimmick to increase fly line sales. Of course, it probably depends a great deal on how much you use it, but I have some fly lines on reels that I used daily that are well over twenty years old, and they still perform great. I like to think it's because I take good care of them. While I'm not very good at cleaning my fly line each season, I am very good at making sure I never put a reel full of wet line back in its reel bag. Moisture is not a friend of the fly-fisher. A general rule of thumb is that you should never store anything wet. One of my post fishing trip rituals is stripping off the portion of line that was in the water most of the day and just letting it dry on the floor overnight. The next day, I will reel up all the loose line and it's all nice and dry for the next fishing trip. If I'm fishing on consecutive days, I may not always do this, but I will always try to make sure the reel is never left in a bag wet.

3. **You really should never put a wet bamboo rod in its rod sleeve and case.** You may be thinking, "But I don't get my rod wet." If that's the case no worries. But if you're ever fishing a bamboo rod in the rain, which many of us do sometimes, you'd better thoroughly dry the entire rod before storing it. Bamboo can rot, and that's exactly what it will do if you leave it in its sleeve wet for an extended period of time. Flies are relatively cheap. Fly lines, not so much. But an expensive bamboo rod ruined by wood rot will make a grown man cry.

4. **You really should store your boot waders hanging upside down on a boot rack.** This really applies only to the minority of us who prefer boot waders to sock waders. The new materials waders are made with these days are much more crack resistant than the ones I grew up using; in those days, I could always count on cracks showing up along the folds. If you hang them up upside down, you eliminate any folds and your waders will last much longer. Another good reason to store them this way is to allow air to enter into the wader all the way up to the sole of the boot, which also helps with odor. Now you may be asking yourself right now why I still use boot waders instead of the more popular socks with a wading boot. The answer is simple: speed and convenience. If I'm fishing with a buddy who has to put on his waders and then his wading boots, and then lace them up, I can have at least a dozen-cast head start on him by just simply slipping into my boots, tightening up the wading belt, and walking out to the water. I will use sock waders when I'm fishing those faraway places that require air travel, because they pack much better, but as a rule I will always take my boot waders whenever I can.

5. **You really should buy a lifetime fishing license while you're young.** This piece of advice obviously comes too late for some readers, but if you have children or grandchildren who love to fish, it makes the perfect gift. I purchased one for my son at a young age, and he was delighted beyond measure. Now he's always ready to fish with me at the drop of a hat. One of the early-season rituals I always dreaded was having to find a place to purchase a fishing license and then making the drive and waiting in line to get one. When I get the

urge to make my first fishing trip of the year, the last thing I want to do is spend time away from the water to buy a license. So, much too late in life, I finally made the one-time effort and purchased a lifetime license, and now I avoid this yearly hassle. It was a one-time investment that I've never regretted.

6. **You really should never be reluctant to ask someone who's having better success than you what he or she is using.** Pride is a silly trait that all of us have to some degree, but in excess, it has consequences. At one point in my life, I was always a little embarrassed to ask; but I realized that in reality, it was the ultimate compliment—one that most fishermen understood. And most seemed more than happy to oblige. Oh, I would imagine there may be the occasional jerk that will give you the snub, but I can't recall that ever happening to me. I feel sorry for those guys, because all they're really doing is exposing their insecurity. I'm a much better fisherman today because I will make the ask, and in the process, I will have added to my knowledge of the sport. Sometimes the person I've asked was so flattered as to give me the fly he or she had been using—a pay-it-forward type of deal. And that generous behavior has often led me to do the same thing. As Frank Burns once said in the hit TV comedy *M*A*S*H*, "It's nice to be nice to the nice."

7. **You really should always listen to the folks working in the fly shop.** Once again, pride will sometimes keep you from doing the smart thing. People who work in fly shops are as passionate about fly-fishing as you are, and they certainly know the local water better than you do. This never was more apparent to me than during a trip I took with Cousin A. B. and friend Chuck

Nithman to the Taneycomo tailwater near Branson, Missouri. Upon a visit to the local fly shop, we asked the common question, "What are they hitting?" and the employee we talked to was quick to point out a tiny red nymph pattern that was made locally. Well, I knew I had something very similar in my fly vest that should work just as well or even better and thought I'd save myself the two bucks for each fly. A. B. and Chuck listened and bought the patterns he recommended, and guess who got into fish later that day? Not me.

Chuck, sensing my frustration, and probably suffering from a sore arm from all the nice browns he had caught, offered me his rig; and sure enough, I got into some action using his fly rod rigged with that custom-made red midge nymph. I'm usually pretty good about following the advice of the local experts, because they are right about 90 percent of the time, but I sure paid the price that day for thinking I knew as much as the locals did.

8. **You really should follow the golden rule on the water.** The vast majority of fly-fishers I've encountered do an excellent job of treating others like they'd like to be treated, but there is the occasional inconsiderate angler that will Al Capone his way into your fishing territory. I've never really known a tactful way of confronting such a person in this situation, because to do so would be an unpleasant experience at best, and I didn't come to paradise to have a personal confrontation with any human being. I get enough of those opportunities at work, and this ain't work. So I typically will just let it go and maybe move on to another spot—not because I'm a wimp, but because it's just not worth it. I did confront someone once who had a collapsible fish-basket full

of trout he had caught in a catch-and-release area, but this was only because I'm not sure I could have lived with myself for watching the law being broken and not doing something about it. It wasn't pleasant, but it was the right thing to do.

9. **You really should never make a cast without checking your leader for abrasions and wind knots.** I also talk about wind knots in chapter 4. None of us want to take the time to undo these pesky things or tie on new tippet material, but the margin of error is already small enough in the fish's favor, and we don't need to be increasing his odds any. Abrasions can be equally lethal to an otherwise healthy tippet, but in their case it's always best just to tie on new line. Tippet rings have made this process a much easier task and are one of the most welcomed innovations that have come about recently. Besides the increased potential of losing a prize fish, I also worry about him swimming around with a fly in his mouth connected to a few feet of monofilament or fluorocarbon.

10. **You really should always have a Walmart bag in your fly vest.** Of course this can just as easily be a Target or Dollar General Store bag, but the point is to leave the area you're fishing better than you found it, and without a bag of some type, it becomes a little bit more difficult to free your area from the trash left by others. The pockets in your pants and vest can carry only so much trash. I will never, for the life of me, understand how some people think they are above policing their own trash, but evidently they think they are a privileged class of folks and it's up to the rest of us to take care of them.

11. **You really should respect the horn.** I discuss this topic in greater detail in my first book, explaining how I narrowly escaped an unexpected float trip down the river in my waders below the Fort Gibson Dam because I kept thinking I had more time to fish than I really did. I learned that day that the warning horn is something you don't want to play games with. The problem with water releases is that they often trigger feeding behavior and you just don't want to give up the spot where you've been catching some fish. The bottom line here is that when the horn sounds, warning you of a water release, be aware of what is about to happen and plan for going to higher ground on the same side of the river where your vehicle is parked.

12. **You really should pay lightning its proper respect.** Similar to water releases of man-made dams, Mother Nature has her own attractive hazards, and they're called storm fronts. I love fishing right before a storm, especially for largemouth bass. I can think of no better remedy for a slumping lake or pond than to time it perfectly and be on the water just before a spring or summer storm. Unfortunately, lightning often accompanies a storm, and that's where fishermen can get themselves into trouble. Graphite rods are great conductors of electricity, so enough said on that subject. Just as football games are cancelled or delayed as soon as the first lightning strike is spotted, fishermen should cancel or delay any further fishing until the storm has passed and the lightning has stopped. As a rule of thumb, I'd recommend following the same policy that was used at the last college football game I attended during a thunderstorm, and that is to not resume fishing until thirty minutes after the last visible lightning flash.

13. **You really should go small when fish aren't hitting.** My good friend and fishing buddy Bob Verboon always tells me to go a size smaller when the trout are not hitting. If that doesn't produce anything, go even smaller, and keep it up until you fished the smallest fly in your box. I've found Bob's rule also applies to warm-water species, such as bass. Fortunately for fly-fishers, the smaller you go, the easier it is to cast.

14. **You really should fish the windy side of the lake or pond.** Wind is the nemesis of fly anglers. Casting is difficult and often very frustrating, but if you can master fly-casting in windy conditions, you can add a lot of fish to your fishing logs. In still-water fisheries, such as ponds and lakes, the fish seem to gather on the windy side, and that's always the first place I'll try. I especially love windy points. The explanation I often hear for this phenomenon is that baitfish become disoriented and are easy prey in turbulent water. Insects are often blown in to the windy shorelines as well, which can initiate a feeding frenzy. Additionally, wave action breaks up light penetration, which makes it more difficult for fish to see you, meaning they are therefore less likely to spook, especially in clear water. So I find it a little amusing when I'm told by some of my fishing buddies that they'd like to go fishing with me tomorrow but, according to the weather forecast, it's going to be too windy. I interpret that same weather forecast as meaning it's going to be a great day to go fishing!

15. **You really should always expect the unexpected.** This is just another way of saying you should always be alert and ready. This includes situations like (1) the short strike and the very end of your retrieve when a fish comes from out of nowhere to charge your bait

just as you're getting ready to pick the line up and make another cast; (2) Fishing mud-stained water that you think can't possibly hold fish (I've caught some huge bass in the muddiest water you can imagine, and I'm still shocked every time it happens); (3) When you haven't had a strike all day and just when you decide to look at some beautiful scenery, your strike indicator disappears and you lose a fish because you weren't paying attention; and (4) Fishing in adverse weather conditions where you are cold and miserable and think the fish are feeling the same way until a monster lets you know he isn't necessarily feeling the same way. To me, that's what makes fishing exciting. You just never know for sure what's going to happen with each cast, which is why one of the most common lies we often hear in our sport is "Just one more cast!"

16. **You really should take a kid fishing.** For our sport to survive in generations to come, I think it is the responsibility of us who dearly love to fish to get the next generation involved as well. There is nothing more rewarding than the look of excitement on a ten-year-old's face when he or she pulls in that first fish. Taking someone from a younger generation and teaching him or her how to fish plants a seed that can grow into a passion that lasts a lifetime. When you leave this earth someday, you should feel confident that, because of your efforts, you have replaced yourself with at least one person (ideally more) who will someday be as passionate about the sport as you are and, in turn, will someday teach others the love of fishing as well. There are organizations like PETA who think fishing should be banned altogether, and our only hope to make sure that never happens is to invest our time and effort in

our youth. So give the gift of fishing to a youngster who can carry it on for one more generation.

At one time, my daughter Kari showed some early signs of becoming a devoted fishing partner, but she had an experience that I don't think she really got over. Kari was just ten years old, and we were living in Cache, Oklahoma. She was fishing with her older brother, Jim, in Rock Creek, a beautiful stream in our neighborhood that flowed out of the Wichita Mountains just north of our house. On her own, she hooked a really nice largemouth bass and asked Jim to help her land it. Her side of the story describes Jim as bungling the attempt to lift the fish out of the water and the fish getting off. While I'm sure her brother's version might differ somewhat regarding how everything went down, Kari was still devastated and wanted so much to bring the prize catch home to show her dad. I don't think she ever recovered from that experience. As I write about in chapter 5, "Oh, How They All Still Hurt," I think this one hurt so bad that her passion for the sport dwindled from that point on. However, in all fairness, I think her interest in basketball, softball, gymnastics, cheerleading, piano, and dance may have played a significant role as well. I mean, you can only be involved in so many extracurricular activities, and Kari always wanted to do them all. As an adult, however, she did give me three wonderful grandsons, Nathan, Noah, and Nicholas, who always want to go fishing with Grandpa, so it's all good. Nonetheless, I can still say with great pride that my son Jim and nephew Dolph have both become passionate and skilled fly anglers and are two confirmed contributions I will take credit for in developing the next generation of fly-fishers. Doing the math, I calculate that I've replaced myself plus one! Can you say you've done at least as much to make sure our beloved sport continues to prosper in the future?

My son Jim and a nice largemouth bass caught
on a #1/0 Olive Articulated Leech.

My nephew Dolph and a nice cutthroat trout
caught on a #18 Purple Flying Ant.

CHAPTER 3

DARN! I ALMOST WAS!

Every little boy who hits a home run, immediately after crossing home plate and receiving all the accolades from his teammates, automatically begins to have visions of playing in game seven of the World Series and hitting the game-winning homer. For me that moment came in the seventh grade while I was attending Spring Valley School, a little dependent school district in Payne County, Oklahoma. We were playing our archrival, Pleasant View, another dependent district just a few miles away. I hit a ball that sailed well over the left fielder's head and bounced all the way back to the swing set just west of the schoolhouse. I remember the feeling of exuberance I had as I watched the left fielder racing all the way back to try to retrieve it before it reached a dusty country road, and it is truly something that I will never forget. I immediately knew I was destined to be the next kid from Oklahoma to play center field for the New York Yankees—the next Mickey Mantle. As it turned out, Bobby Murcer, from Oklahoma City, became that guy and not me.

Heck, I would spend hours in front of Mom's vanity mirror in my parents' bedroom working on the most intimidating batting stance I could come up with that would surely strike fear in the hearts and minds of opposing pitchers. I even learned how to be a switch hitter just like Mickey, and I spent hours on both sides of a makeshift plywood home plate outside our barn, hitting black walnuts that had dropped from a tree nearby and watching them sail over the fence that separated the house from our chicken yard. Dad would get upset because his lawn mower would often pick up the walnuts and sometimes throw them at another family member who might be in the vicinity, but I interpreted that as a true testament to my prowess as a future big-league home run hitter. Each of those walnuts represented a home run!

Of course, it wasn't long before I realized that a career in the major leagues was not my destiny and that I would have to decide on a career that was better suited to my God-given talents. For the vast majority of us, that grasp of reality comes pretty early in life; for others unwilling to give up on the dream, it comes much later. My good friend Steve Moody, who had dreams of playing wide receiver in the NFL, made it all the way to the junior college level, playing for Northern Oklahoma College in Tonkawa, Oklahoma. He liked to relate that his moment of reality came when he noticed that some of the defensive backs he was playing against could run backward faster than he could run forward. Thus ended his dreams of becoming the next Fred Biletnikoff.

Okay, so what about fishing as a possible livelihood? I mean, I was pretty darned good at it based on the all the local success I had on our neighborhood farm ponds. Perhaps I could be the next Vernon Roscoe "Gadabout" Gaddis and host my own TV fishing show every Saturday like he did. I never missed *The Flying Fisherman*. Gadabout would hop into his airplane and travel all over the country showing us some of the best fishing spots that his Piper Tri-Pacer could reach. For someone who rarely got an opportunity to leave the farm, let alone Oklahoma, being a TV host for a fishing show had as much appeal as playing for the New York Yankees—maybe even more. Of course, I would also have to learn how to fly an airplane like Gadabout, but that could surely be arranged somehow. What fun it would be taking his place when he retired.

If that didn't work out, I had an alternative plan to be a local celebrity like Joe Krieger. Mr. Krieger hosted *The Joe Krieger Show* on KOTV Channel 6 in Tulsa, which we could barely pick up in Stillwater, but through all the fuzz and static on the TV screen, I watched each episode. I learned a great deal from that show. Joe would go all over the region and bring back exciting film footage of spots I had never heard of in Oklahoma, as well as locations in some neighboring states that were relatively close to home. I loved that show and to this day credit him for teaching me how to fish plastic worms. He was an absolute genius at using the Fliptail Daddy plastic worm. Unlike the dream of becoming the starting center fielder for the Yankees, the dream of being able to make a living as a professional fisherman was difficult for me to abandon, and it wasn't until I reached my late forties when two specific incidents happened that convinced me I'd better stick to education as a sure and safe way to pay the bills. Being a celebrity TV host just wasn't going to be in the cards.

The first incident that involved an "almost was" that I was convinced would launch me into being the next Mel Krieger of fly-casting video fame was a lost opportunity to teach Miss America how to fly-fish. While working at the Oklahoma Department of Career and Technology Education, I had the opportunity to become acquainted with Shawntel Smith, Miss America for 1996, who was from Muldrow, Oklahoma. Shawntel was dating Chad Foster, the TV host for ESPN2's

Fly Fish America, at the time, and she wanted to surprise him with her skills as a fly-fisher. It had to be only a matter of time before Chad would surely choose a romantic fly-fishing venue on a scenic river somewhere where they could fly-fish together as a part of their courtship. The only problem was that she didn't know the first thing about fly-fishing. The stars began to align for me when we learned at the State Career-Tech Department that Shawntel wanted to select as her platform during her reign as Miss America, the newly passed federal legislation titled School-To-Work, which in Oklahoma was to be administered by the Oklahoma Department of Career-Tech. Shawntel's mother was a vocational home economics teacher and probably had some influence on her decision. Regardless, the school-to-work initiative was a very worthy program—one that could certainly benefit from the national exposure she would be able to give it as Miss America.

Well, word got out within the state agency that I was a fly-fisher and that I might be the perfect guy to give her fly-fishing lessons so she could adequately handle a fly rod by the time she and Chad eventually got on the water together. Of course, when I was asked if I'd be willing to be her instructor, I jumped all over it, and a date was set for me to teach her how to fly-fish. I immediately began doing some research and developed what I thought was a great curriculum and organized it into a three-ring binder that would serve as a textbook and reference guide for her to keep. After all, I was a former high school vocational teacher, so I knew a thing or two about teaching skills to students; I just hadn't ever done it on the subject of fly-fishing. I was pretty excited about it and also about the possibility of meeting her boyfriend, Chad, who I hoped would be impressed with the great job I did in developing her fly-fishing skills. Heck, I thought he might even ask me to be a guest on his TV show someday, and who knows where it might have gone from there. But a few days before the lessons were to begin, Shawntel came down with the flu, and we had to postpone the class. Of course, you can imagine how busy her schedule was as the reigning Miss America, and another date that would work with her schedule could never be found. I heard later that they had broken up, so an opportunity to teach Miss America how to fly-fish never presented itself. But still, it made for a pretty neat "almost was."

A second opportunity to become a TV celebrity came from my former brother-in-law, Rod Smith, who worked for the Oklahoma Department of Wildlife Conservation (ODWC). When Rod heard about the successful sight fishing I had been doing with carp on Taylor Lake near Rush Springs, Oklahoma, he informed fellow ODWC staffer Larry Cofer, who hosted an outdoors show on local television station KSWO-TV Channel 7, in Lawton, Oklahoma. Larry contacted me and said he'd like to meet me at Taylor Lake to take some film and do an interview for his show. Of course, I eagerly accepted his invitation and immediately began to plan my trip based on the past successes I had on that lake sight fishing for common carp. This was going to be my second chance at TV fame and glory! But then I made the cardinal mistake of thinking this was a sure deal. I had never before been skunked at Taylor Lake fishing for carp, so my confidence was off the charts. But as I've found out many times in the past, if there is a sure way to anger the fishing gods, it's to be a little bit too cocky.

With that thought in the back of my mind, I did my best to resist the temptation to already see myself on TV screens in homes all over southwestern Oklahoma and north central Texas. I went to my closet and laid out my classiest fishing shirt, best-fitting fishing pants, and sharpest-looking ball cap to wear for the show. I selected my most expensive fly rig that would look great on camera and headed out the door to meet Larry at Taylor Lake.

When I got there, I found him to be one of the nicest people I had ever met, and he carefully explained that he would be asking a lot of questions while he was filming me fish. "Okay," he said, "where do you want to start?" I knew exactly where I wanted to begin and exactly the pattern I wanted to tie on, so that part was easy. I selected some shoreline flats that were bordered by long stretches of cattails, where I had always seen plenty of cruising carp with many active feeders making their signature mud puffs while looking for food. Using my best stealth techniques, I began wading the hard-packed sandy bottom shoreline in about two or three feet of crystal-clear water and began my search. But on this day, they were nowhere to be found. I guess I had angered the gods, and they were letting me know who was really in charge. But the day was young, and there was plenty of water left to fish, so I viewed it as only a temporary setback.

We fished all day without a single take. Unbelievable! I felt this couldn't be happening. How embarrassing. Larry, being the perfect gentleman, said, "Well, I've got a lot of great b-roll for the show, but I need to have some footage of you catching a fish. Let's come back next week, and I'm betting this won't happen to you twice in a row." I agreed, but with only a fraction of the confidence I'd had that morning.

We scheduled a second day, and I met Larry at the same spot, but this time Rod also met us there. It was really good to see him again, as I had always considered him to be a great friend in addition to being my brother-in-law for over thirty years.

I don't even want to write about what happened the rest of that day, but to add to the humiliation, I got skunked for a second time. I'm not sure whom I felt sorrier for—me for my poor performance on the water for a second straight week, or Rod because he was the one who recommended to Larry that he do a show about me carp fishing. I didn't have the nerve to ask for a third opportunity. I had already wasted enough of Larry's time, and by this time, my self-confidence had hit rock bottom anyway, and I wasn't sure whether I'd ever catch another carp on a fly rod again.

But if you're going to be good at anything, you have to get through the hard times and just keep on trudging, and that's what I did. I eventually got my confidence back in my ability to catch carp and had success the very next time I went to Taylor Lake, but I was by myself and there wasn't any pressure. Some folks are meant for the bright lights and others aren't. Once I accepted that reality, I was perfectly content just to be out on the water and enjoy fishing again for the pure joy of what each trip naturally brings in terms of mystery and excitement.

It took me a long time to forgive the entire carp species for the humiliation they had bestowed on me that fateful day, but I eventually got over it. Those two days of unproductive fishing on Taylor Lake wound up making me respect them as game fish more than ever. On those two particular days, the carp clearly had a decisive victory, but sometimes you just have to tip your hat to your opponent and say, "Good for you this time, but let's get after it again sometime soon!"

CHAPTER 4

WIND KNOTS AND OTHER IRRITANTS

As I've gotten older, I've noticed myself beginning to question things that I really never thought about much before. Maybe it's because since I've retired I just have more time to contemplate stuff. For example, why is the person who invests your money called a broker? Why don't sheep shrink when they get wet? Why do we park our cars on driveways but drive them on parkways? And if you could drive a car faster than the speed of light and you turned on your headlights, would they even come on? While those are all kind of silly thoughts, most of my ponderables these days focus on the topic of fishing in general and fly-fishing in particular.

As a senior fly-fisher, I have become less tolerant, it seems, of irritating things that always seem to happen to me at the worst time. For example, why is it that my fly line always seeks the only pointed rock on the ground where I'm standing to wrap itself around? Or it might be a little stick near my feet that was nearly invisible before my WF8F found it. I mean, there are a million other places fly line could nicely lie while

I'm trying to make a cast, but it seems to always find an obstacle in one form or another to prevent me from shooting out all the line I have on the ground.

And then there's the challenge of fishing from a boat—especially one with a bow-mounted trolling motor on the casting deck like those you see in bass boats. I actually had a bass boat at one time and tried fly-fishing from it, and I never did find a way to keep the line from wrapping itself around some part of the foot control or anything I tried to cover it with. I finally gave up and sold the boat.

Fly line management was never more important than the time I was fishing for false albacore in the outer banks of North Carolina with a guide. False albacore are incredibly strong fish with blazing speed. When you hook on to one of those guys, it's like hooking on to a freight train, and your drag will smoke from the many fast runs they make. I think I literally wore out the disc drag on my fly reel after a day of dealing with these brutes, because it never again worked quite as smoothly after that trip. I have no regrets though. Replacing a reel is just the price of having great fun catching a lot of fish with tremendous muscle and heart. Besides, it gave me something to talk about to my freshwater fishing buddies when I got home. The guide told me to always look at my feet as I was stripping in the line because anything wrapped around the fly line on the floor of the boat was going into the water, including me! He wasn't kidding, and I took great pains to follow his advice after I connected with my first fish and felt the power of that first long run. But all day long, I just knew my fly line wanted to throw me into the ocean for making it strain so much in doing battle with these powerful fish.

And let's not forget about those trees that seem too far behind us to matter when making our back cast, only to find out that they are at the perfect distance for our fly to find.

It appears that, for some unknown reason, fly-fishers do a pretty good job of estimating the distance in front of them to a feeding fish but have an innate ability to misjudge distance behind them. Losing a fly on the back cast to a weed is really frustrating. With a tree you can usually go back and find the fly in a tree branch, but if a bunch of tall grass or a weed snaps off your fly, well, that's a different story altogether. Should you ever be foolish enough to think you can just walk back and find that fly in the blade of grass or the weed that robbed you of it, forget it, even if you carefully measured the distance of your back cast and walked to that area where you knew the fly just had to be. Interestingly enough, you usually can find the fly of some other unfortunate angler who lost his or hers in the same exact way. Is it possible that the flies that we so painstakingly tie at our fly-tying desks can actually acquire the skill of flight once they escape the bondage of our tippets? I, for one, certainly can't prove that they don't develop that ability. Do feathers that once flew when they were a vital part of a pheasant or duck magically become reincarnated into some other form of flying creature? These are all questions that plague me, especially when things are not going well on the water. And why is it that the fly you'll lose on that fatal back cast is the only fly you've had any success with that day and the last one of its kind in your fly vest? Maybe, just maybe, success in catching fish is the qualifying factor for the fly to be broken off so it can earn its freedom! Ladies and gentlemen, we have many unexplained cosmic forces working against us as fly-fishers, and I'm not done yet pointing them all out.

The title of this chapter specifically mentions wind knots. I wouldn't mind occasionally getting these pesky little things if they didn't reduce the strength of my leader. But why something as simple as an overhand knot, which is what they really are, substantially reduces the strength of your line while the more elaborate knots with many more twists and turns—like the improved clinch, the Palomar, and the Duncan loop—do not, is beyond my comprehension. It doesn't make any sense. The thing I hate most about wind knots is that they let the world know that you have poor form as a fly-caster, as their appearance is due more to the misuse of applied physics than how hard the wind is blowing. I have calculated that for every wind knot your leader has at the end of the day, you lose about 10 percent of your credibility as an accomplished fly angler. So as you leave your favorite fishery with your buddies and head for that long-awaited bourbon in a tin cup to swap stories about the fish you caught or the fish you lost, and you have five wind knots in your leader and your buddy sees them, rest assured you've lost 50 percent of your credibility as a fly-fisher! That means half of what you say that evening won't be taken very seriously.

Because of this, it is vital that you remove your wind knots as soon as they appear, not only because their presence increases your risk of breaking off a good fish but also because you always want to project the appearance of being a talented fly-fisher. And don't kid yourself; there will always be those fly-anglers who are looking for ways they can discredit you, and wind knots are the first place they look.

Another frustrating thing about wind knots is trying to untie them once they've gone unnoticed for a while and have tightened up. While personally I rarely get these nasty little bastards (wink, wink), the rare times that I do, my first approach is to take the eyelet-cleaning spike that is built into my nipper and see whether I can penetrate the point somewhere into the knot itself in an effort to loosen it. The smaller the leader or tippet material, the more difficult this becomes. I will try to strategically position the knot on my thumbnail and gently drive the point into the knot against the surface of my nail. Sometimes it slips off my nail and the hook penetrates the skin of my thumb. That can be very painful and is a good reason why all of us should make sure we stay current with our tetanus vaccinations. Sometimes I finally get the point through the knot so I can untie it, but in the course of doing so, I fatally fray the leader, reducing the strength to less than what it would have been if I had left the knot untouched in the first place. Of course, leaving the knot there is never a good option, because somebody might see it, and then you're really screwed. Wind knots rank right up there with leaky waders, shoreside trash, and mosquitos as my most dreaded irritants.

And while we're on the subject of wind, why is it that it always seems to blow at hurricane strength during the week I have a fishing trip planned? Before I retired, I always had to plan my fishing trips around an insanely busy work schedule. It always seemed that the very day before my trip, the weather would turn bad for a week, and the most common culprit was wind in the 20–30 mph category. Now, personally, I prefer a little ripple on the water because I think it makes for more active fish, but the wind we typically get in Oklahoma is of the gale variety. I'm convinced that one of the reasons my alma mater, Oklahoma State University, is one of the blue bloods of collegiate golf is our team's ability to play effectively in windy conditions. They achieve this skill because that's nearly all they see on their home course, Karsten Creek. And while I haven't done the research, I would bet that most of the eleven NCAA championship titles the school has were won in windy weather and our guys knew how to play in those kinds of conditions better than those boys from Princeton or Stanford. A common saying around here is "If you can't play golf in the wind, then give up the sport." It's the same for fly-fishing in the Midwest. If you can't or don't like casting a fly on windy days, then you're better off taking up bowling, billiards, darts, or some other indoor sport. But on the positive side, excessive wind is one of the few irritants that I've found a remedy for. It's called retirement. Nowadays, when the weather is perfect, I just gather all my gear and go fish. It still poses a bit of a problem for those times when I need to plan trips a month or more in advance, because when I do, I can almost count on a record-setting gale for the entire time I'm out on the water.

Leaky waders are a very common irritant among all fly-fishers—but one that also has an easy remedy: just make sure you have a backup pair with you on all your fishing trips. There is nothing more uncomfortable than sloshing around all day with wet socks and freezing inside a pair of leaky waders. Early in my fly-fishing journey, I noticed that if the only pair of waders I had for the trip was going to leak, it was for sure going to happen on the first day of the trip. That way I could be miserable for each and every day of the entire trip. Would I ever spring a leak on the last day? Never! I eventually wised up to this inevitable situation and bought a spare pair, and now I never leave home without them.

Actually, now I kind of look forward to my waders leaking, because it gives me an excuse to go out and buy some new ones constructed with all the latest features and made from some new space-age material invented by a NASA scientist to prepare astronauts for space exploration. Of course, astronauts never have to deal with earthly things like sharp rocks, briar patches, and barbed wire fences, which are kryptonite to waders; but then, a leak in one's space suit is far more hazardous to one's health when roaming the galaxy than a leak in one's waders when roaming the Rio Grande! Back when I was younger and fishing on a very tight budget, I used to always try to patch my waders, and I still do in emergency situations, but now that I'm in a better position financially, I just make a fun trip to my local outfitter and get some new ones. This is one of the nice advantages of being an empty nester.

And speaking of wading, for those of us who love to fish farm ponds and small lakes, there's always the challenge of sinking knee-deep into the mud and muck so many of our silted-in farm ponds and lakes are plagued with. So many productive farm ponds are nearly impossible to wade from shore. I've lost too many paddle pushers (side boot fins) that were attached to my waders just trying to get through all that yucky stuff in an attempt to get to deeper water with my float tube. My cousin A. B. found a remedy to this problem by simply drilling a hole through the boot heel and the paddle pusher housing and stringing a wire through it to secure the pusher to the boot heel. I never lost another one after I did that. I love irritants that have fixes.

Another wading-related irritant that, in my opinion, has no real effective solution, is the thin, slimy moss attached to the rocks on the bottom of some rivers. The worst of these is the Lower Mountain Fork in Oklahoma right below the reregulation dam. While boots with studs and a good wading stick do help, you still feel like you're flirting with disaster each time you take a step, particularly if the water flow is faster than normal.

And how about kids throwing rocks in the water? Does that ever happen to you? In some of the places I fish that have easy road access, and are frequented by families with small children just enjoying a day in the outdoors, this happens more often than you would think it should. I get the fascination small kids have with throwing rocks in the water and hearing the loud kerplunk they make on impact. Heck, we all did the same thing when we were young. But parents, have a clue about what it does to the fishing when anglers are present. And show some respect for folks like us who buy the fishing licenses and join organizations like Trout Unlimited and Federation of Flyfishers, who all are responsible for channeling tons of resources toward conservation efforts to ensure that you have those pristine rivers to throw rocks into in the first place. There is always plenty of river with rocks nearby to do that type of thing where there are no anglers around. And oh! Here's an idea. Instead of taking those kids to a river to throw rocks, buy them a rod and reel, and teach them how to fish!

Another irritant is the illegal angler: the one who keeps fish in a catch-and-release area, uses barbed hooks in a barbless zone, or has more fish on his or her stringer than the legal limit allows. It's always unpleasant to point these things out to these folks, and you never know what kind of reaction you're going to get. Of course, we've all probably experienced the angler that thinks he or she is entitled to your fishing spot and just kind of muscles up to you, nearly shoulder to shoulder. There is nothing illegal about it, I guess, but it is certainly a violation of fly-fishing ethics.

Anglers who don't treat the fish they've caught with the proper respect are also disturbing to me, particularly in the catch-and-release areas, where the main idea is to return the fish to the water in a healthy condition. I've seen people drag the fish up on shore over rocks, sand, and mud; unhook them; and then toss them back into the water like those same kids throwing rocks that I mentioned above. If you don't have a net and are forced to take the fish out of the water, please be careful with this precious resource and gently return it to the water and revive it if necessary before you physically let go of it.

While it is not an annoyance as much as it is an amusement, I find a lot of paradox in watching a so-called sportsman who may be a top money winner on the BASS Pro Tour, wearing a clown suit cluttered with logos while doing a television show.

This guy I was watching on TV the other day yelled and screamed the instant he hooked a fish with a rod that had the action of a broomstick and with a reel that resembled a winch on the front of a Jeep Rubicon and using fishing line that had the same pound test as a good piece of cattle rope. He would then proceed to skate the fish on top of the water until it got yanked into the boat. He then held it by the lower jaw, mouth extended to maximum, to show off to his TV audience. Finally, he flipped this proud creature of God into the water so he could quickly do the same thing to another bass. And the whole time he's doing it, he's screaming at the top of his lungs as if he just dunked on LeBron James. "Look at me! Look at what I just did! I caught a fish!" I don't get all the dramatics, but I guess that type of behavior has an audience who enjoy it. I just miss the classy old guys like Jimmy Houston, Roland Martin, Rick Clunn, and Bill Dance, who in their day would win more than their fair share of the tournaments, professionally do their television shows, and always pay the sport its proper respect, without all the theatrics. But professional fishing isn't the only sport that has been plagued by this type of behavior. I also miss the sight of Barry Sanders simply handing the football to the official after breaking half a dozen tackles to score a touchdown, and then trotting off to the sidelines as if it were just another day at the office.

Getting a hook buried in your body past the barb is probably one of the most painful irritants a fisherman has to deal with. I've personally had it happen to me on six occasions. Because these human hook-ups are so painful, I vividly remember every single incident and the chain of events that caused each one and what I had to do to remove the hook. I still have scars to show for some of them. I won't go into detail about every errant time I caught myself instead of a fish, but suffice it to say I prepared for the worst, as this is one of the hazards of this beloved avocation of mine. Most of them occurred back when I was fishing with conventional gear and my lures usually came armed with treble hooks and barbs. The first time it happened, I was fishing in a farm pond and got hung up in a willow tree with a Rooster Tail spinner. After realizing that I could probably kiss the lure good-bye, I positioned my spinning rod parallel to the ground so it wouldn't need to bend and pulled straight back. All of a sudden, the willow tree released the lure, but only after the limb it was hooked to acted like a hunting bow and propelled the metal lure straight at my head like an arrow. The treble hook wound up in the corner of my left eye, just barely missing the eyeball. Close call! The skin in that part the face is extremely soft and pliable, so it wasn't coming out. I was in my early twenties and didn't have any experience with this sort of thing, so at the urging of my wife, I went to the emergency room to see what they would do about it. Their procedure was pretty simple, the doctor simply snipped off the point of the hook and pulled it out. Heck, I could have done that and saved myself the cost of a doctor's bill and kept on fishing. I just didn't think about it. I guess that's why physicians go through all that schooling. Still, I was a little disappointed that he couldn't save my Rooster Tail. It was my favorite one, and those things don't grow on trees. They just get hung up in them.

From that point on, I have made a hat or ball cap an essential part of my fishing uniform. I now keep my head down with the bill of my cap covering my face as I make the pull on any snagged lure or fly. The ER doc did have a sense of humor about it and said that if I liked the look of the Rooster Tail in the corner of my eye, he could pierce it for me. That way I could change it out to match the color of my shirt. Today people are piercing all parts of their bodies, so having a shiny fishing lure in the corner of one eye might start the latest fashion craze in body piercing. Later I found a set of earrings made of fishing flies at a fly shop and thought of that Rooster Tail story. I purchased them for my wife, Cindy, as a Christmas gift. It disappoints me she doesn't wear them more, as she is definitely one of my better catches!

Now we come to the irritant that probably bothers me more than anything else, and it's those inconsiderate fishermen who trash our lakes and streams. They must be lazy or arrogant, or maybe they're just plain stupid. How can they not feel guilty going to a pristine area and leaving it full of their trash? Or maybe they think that an empty power bait jar actually looks pretty good setting next to the shoreline. What is going through their minds when they leave a tangled mess of monofilament in the brush, just waiting to ambush an innocent animal (if it's on land) or a fish (if it's left in the water)? I honestly don't get it. Human behavior can be so disappointing sometimes. One reason I love our breed of fishermen is that I can honestly say I have never seen a fly-fisher leave trash on the water. And more often than not, I see many of our long-rod brethren pick up trash that isn't theirs and put it in a bag they brought just for that purpose. Hats off to Trout Unlimited and Fishpond for teaming up to promote a clever little vessel they call a piopod, with "pio" being an acronym for "pack it out." It's a microtrash container. I got mine through Trout Unlimited, and it is the handiest little gadget that slips right on your belt or fly vest and ingeniously stores discarded monofilament, wrappers, cigarette butts, and the like until you can get to a public waste container to dispose of it properly. It makes picking up trash fun and an integral part of the fly-fishing experience. What a great piece of equipment every fisherman should have on his or her person. It should be just as important to have one with you as your trusty nipper.

I'll end this chapter with a little story that I have to admit may have been a practical joke gone a tad bit too far. I was on a wilderness float trip with some really great guys to the Middle Fork of the Salmon River in Idaho. To this day, I think it's one of the prettiest rivers I've ever been on. I was taking a break with a fly angler whom I didn't know well but really liked and respected. We got to talking about how beautiful the entire area was and how neither of us had yet to see trash of any kind. We agreed, with a bit of smugness in our tone, that we could tell nobody but fly-fishers probably ever fished this stretch of the river. I then proceeded to finish off my traditional candy of choice during fishing trips, a luscious Zero bar, and wadded the wrapper up and threw it on the ground and started walking off just to see what kind of reaction I would get. I'll never forget the look on his face. It was as if he had witnessed a hit-and-run. He was speechless.

Of course, I quickly told him I was just playing with him, but I'm not sure he thought it was very funny, to say the least, especially after the conversation we just had about the pristine area we were fishing. At any rate, I have to admit that the physical act of throwing that tiny piece of trash on the ground and briefly walking away was a very weird feeling—one I had never experienced before, and I just felt awful about it, even in fun. It made me wonder what kind of person can actually do that for real and not feel as though he or she is doing something wrong. It's one of the mysteries of life that I'm not sure even practicing psychologists and psychiatrists can explain other than by stating it must be a mental disease that some people have.

I imagine irritants will always be a part of fishing as long as the fly reel sings and the trout continue to rise. Maybe it's just part of the charm of our sport to see how well we can tolerate a few annoyances as we engage in our passion. Baseball has its rain delays, golf its sand traps, and track its false starts. Why should fly-fishing be any different?

CHAPTER 5

OH, HOW THEY ALL STILL HURT

I suspect there are very few totally self-actualized anglers out in the real world. You know, the ones who are so secure within themselves that when they go out fishing and lose the fish of a lifetime, they reflect and say to themselves, "Good job, old buddy. What a great time we had testing our skills against each other. You bested me this time, but I'll be back and land you the next time we meet, because I'll be just a little bit smarter." As much as I'd like to believe I'm at that stage in the angler maturation process, the fact is that I still get physically sick to my stomach every time one of those coveted creatures manages to get off before I have an opportunity to take a picture of it with my phone and release it into its environs.

Now, I don't think I'm quite to the mental state described by Steve Duda, editor of *The Flyfish Journal*, who once wrote in a tongue-and-cheek manner, "If my fishing life sucks, the rest of my life probably ain't much better." However, I'm probably closer than I want to be. Evidence for that was just recently refreshed when I lost a seven- to eight-pound largemouth bass on Oklahoma Lake on a fly rod this past fall. I was just sick about it for several days, and if the truth be known, I still am. In fact, lost trophy fish, as infrequent as they have been in my sixty plus years of fishing, still bother me to today, going all the way back to 1960. I can still vividly remember all the details of each missed opportunity for the glory that can only come from landing a prize fish.

A big channel cat that I lost back when I was only twelve years old still stings. It occurred on one of those memorable summer vacation stays at my Uncle Chuck's house in Orlando, Oklahoma. I talk in more detail about those wonderful visits to Uncle Chuck and Aunt Emma's house in chapter 2 of my first book, *If It Were Easy, They'd Call It Catchin'*. On this particular trip to Orlando, my cousin A. B. and I had been hired by Uncle Chuck to tear down an old shed on his property, and the reward for doing so was a little bit of salary. But more important to both A. B. and me than the money was the huge perk of getting to go fishing with our uncle at some prized farm ponds each evening. At that age, both my cousin and I were into catching rather than fishing, and it was important to our self-esteem to have bragging rights in the form of a stringer of fish to take back to clean and eat.

One evening the goal was to bring home some catfish for Aunt Emma to fry for supper. Uncle Chuck took us to a farm that had a series of ponds that were supposed to have some good channel catfish in them. I remember both A. B. and Uncle Chuck catching several nice catfish on minnows in this one beautiful crystal-clear pond. The fish that came from that pond were dark and beautifully colored, and they looked as if they belonged on a fish identification chart published by the Oklahoma Department of Wildlife Conservation. I hadn't caught a single fish yet, probably because my still-developing fishing skills had not yet reached a level that my older cousin had achieved. Tired and frustrated, I made the bold decision to go to a smaller pond directly above the one all of us had been fishing. I told Uncle Chuck of my intentions, and he responded, "Tommy, that pond is just a mud hole—a filter pond for this one—and I don't think there are even any fish in it." Now, normally I listened to every word my uncle said because I admired him so much and thought he was just about the best fisherman in the entire state of Oklahoma. But I was determined to try something different because I was tired of watching everybody catch fish except me, so what did I have to lose?

I hiked to that pond, and sure enough, it was just as Uncle Chuck had described it—muddy and much smaller. Undeterred, I went ahead and cast my bobber and minnow straight out in front of me, and almost immediately my round red-and-white bobber went straight down with authority, and I had a catfish on that was bigger than what I had seen A. B. and my uncle catching. It was almost as if she had been waiting for someone to finally fish the pond where she lived.

The English language is incapable of adequately describing the joy and excitement I felt at that moment. Man, what were they going to say when I brought this four-pound-plus catfish back to where they were fishing? The wisdom they would surely think I had for trying a pond that both my older cousin and uncle thought had no fish. How they would brag on me for having the skills and expertise at such a young age to try a pond they had advised me to avoid, only for me to bring back a fish larger than either one of them had caught! It was almost too much for my young mind to comprehend.

After a hard battle for a considerable length of time, I thought I had her licked and began making progress in reeling her onto shore. I know now that my excitement compromised my good judgement, and I began forcing her in before she was adequately played out. I dragged her out of the water and had her belly just barely on the bank when the strain of her frantic efforts to get free were more than my ten-pound-test monofilament line could stand, and she broke off. Oh my gosh, the dreams I had conjured up in my young mind of taking that fish back for bragging rights were gone in an instant.

In my panic to find a remedy for what was about to be a complete disaster, I did the only thing a normal twelve-year-old would do and immediately dropped my rod and reel and went to my hands and knees to try to fetch her by hand. I actually had my hands on her back, behind the pointed dorsal fin, and was all so close to grabbing her, but she was just too slick-skinned and powerful, and she wiggled her way back to the water. I recall instantly hearing the voice of Jim McKay, the announcer of *ABC's Wide World of Sports*, talking to me from that little TV that all of us have in our minds, saying, "The thrill of victory and the agony of defeat!" Thanks, Mr. McKay! That was just what I needed to hear about then.

I became that skier tumbling out of control down the slope. For my efforts, I was a muddy mess from head to toe, and all I had to show for it was a broken line, a lost snelled hook, and wet muddy jeans, shirt, and shoes. The devastation was just awful. I went back to where Uncle Chuck and A. B. were fishing and had my first opportunity to utter those words that any serious fisherman fears the most: "You should have seen the one that got away." Of course, both A. B. and Uncle Chuck were very empathetic and felt my pain. They could both tell by looking at my mud-stained clothing that something bad had happened, but without evidence, they had only my word that my near catch would have been the biggest catch of the day.

That's a pain that I hoped would never occur again during my fishing journey, but alas, it was just a foretaste of unfortunate experiences yet to come. Of course, no sport is absent of its strikeouts, incomplete passes, or missed easy putts, but that doesn't make any of them less difficult to accept. But nonetheless, if I was going to be a complete fisherman, I needed to experience that feeling of failure and learn how to deal with it in a mature manner—something I'm still working on.

It was about a year later, at age thirteen, that I had a second opportunity to experience that terrible feeling of losing a fish. It was during a family vacation to Roaring River State Park in Cassville, Missouri, with my family. Mom and Dad always enjoyed taking vacations with my uncles and aunts and their families. This trip was with my Uncle Gus and Aunt Sophie and two cousins, Frank and Patti. I had never caught a trout before after trying hard with no success on previous trips and had resigned myself to the notion that such a feat could be accomplished only by adults. I tied on a shad scale Fly Ike (a fly rod version of a Lazy Ike) and unexpectedly hooked my first ever rainbow trout. I had a gallery that day, as Mom and Aunt Sophie were seated in lawn chairs, watching Frank and me fish. Shortly after my hook-up, I heard voices shouting behind me. "Florence, look! Tommy has a fish! Tommy has a fish!" Then, as if both aunts had suddenly become seasoned fishing guides, they began shouting instructions at me: "Don't lose him. Keep a tight line. Don't horse him in." Great, just what I needed—added pressure from my mom and aunt, who knew less about fishing than I did! Similar to the catfish I almost caught with A. B. and Uncle Chuck, I nearly got it on shore, but it, too, got off and wiggled its way back into the river. I was just stunned and about ready to cry. My older cousin Frank, who was fishing a little ways downriver, also had yet to catch a fish, and I had been about to one-up him, but the limp line served as evidence that such bragging was not going to happen on that fateful day. But at least I had two credible witnesses who would testify that I'd had one on and nearly landed it.

A third fish that comes to mind was the first really big largemouth bass I hooked while fishing a farm pond about a mile west of my parents' farm. I was sixteen years old and had just bought my first car, a used green 1959 Opel Rekord that I was so proud of. Now that I had my own vehicle, I would no longer need to depend on transportation provided by A. B. to get to farm ponds that were out of range for my bicycle. This was bound to improve my fishing success exponentially. The day was very windy, with gusts probably close to 20 mph, and I had tied on an a very old and ugly ½-ounce copper spoon that had been given to me by Uncle Chuck during one of our fishing trips. With my spinning reel, I could cast it a country mile with the wind at my back. On one of the first casts, the biggest bass of my life at age sixteen took the tarnished old lure immediately. I estimated her to be in the five- to six-pound range. After the first jump, I knew how big she was, and with all the distance between where I was standing and where she hit, I knew it was going to be a long, hard fight before I would be able to get her to shore. She jumped four more times, and with each jump I had the opportunity to get a better look at her. I began anticipating how proud I was going to be to take her home to show to Mom and Dad. But on the last jump, she shook the spoon, and I was left with that feeling all of us hate—that of a limp line on my rod. That would have been my first lunker bass! The feeling I had of losing that big channel cat with Uncle Chuck and A. B. came flooding back, and even the drive home in my new car didn't change things much. Man, I needed that fish to help with my self-confidence.

By this time, I was well into journaling fish that I had successfully landed, but the one thing I regret not doing in those early days as a boy learning how to be a good angler was journaling the fish I lost. You probably have more opportunity to learn from failures than you do from your successes, but for me, at the time, my failures were just too painful to write about. I still remember some of the more dramatic experiences of lost big fish when I was younger, but many of the details as to what I did wrong on those occasions are lost forever as a learning resource. These days I'm a much better journaler and will also document lost fish because they can provide valuable information as well as important reflective thoughts about each trip.

The loss of a fourth fish that I will always remember occurred on a trip to Cherokee, Oklahoma, to see my first wife's grandparents. Grandad Smith was a passionate angler and, in many ways, made up for my never having the opportunity to know either of my grandfathers before they died. Every time we went to Cherokee, I knew there was going to be a fishing trip to a great farm pond at some point during our visit, so I always looked forward to the two-and-a-half-hour drive to northwestern Oklahoma. His name was William Thomas, and mine was Thomas William, which he always thought was pretty special. The way he'd always wake me up at the crack of dawn to go fishing was to say, "Thomas William, William Thomas is a-calling you. Let's go fishing." I immediately would awake out of my deep slumber wide-eyed and bushy-tailed, ready for some really good fishing.

One morning he took me and my brother-in-law Rod Smith to a huge sand pit pond that had the clearest water in it I'd ever seen in Oklahoma. The only problem was that it was rimmed with heavy vegetation for about the first five to six feet around the entire shoreline. Despite all the shoreline vegetation, I was able to force the ten- to twelve-inch bass I was catching through it without much problem. Then I tied on a jointed purple coach dog Cisco Kid lure and had a hook-up with a six- to seven-pound monster that I knew from the very outset was going to be a real problem landing. After several jumps, I was able to bring her to the edge of the vegetation, and that's when she went deep on me, and all I brought back was a huge five- to six-pound clump of coontail wrapped around my Cisco Kid. Grandad Smith and Rod were nowhere around at the time, so just as with the lost catfish with Uncle Chuck and A. B, there were no witnesses; all I had was a good story to share and the look of a broken heart. By this time, I was married with an infant son and was a little bit more mature, so I was able to handle it a little bit better, but all I could think of on the long drive home was how great it would have been to have landed that fish.

Another lost fish that still rings in my mind is a four-pound smallmouth bass that I hooked years later using a pearl-and-blue Blados Crease Fly on Lake Obabikon in Ontario, Canada. Catching a four-pound smallmouth on a fly rod is quite a prize, and I remember watching from the rear seat in Jim Smith's bass boat as this huge smallie came straight up out of the depths like a guided missile locked in on my Crease Fly. Man, was that ever exciting! After a terrific fight on my 8-weight rig, I had her pretty much whipped and was bringing her in to land so I could get a picture of her when the third person in the boat, Don Duckwall, volunteered to net her. I thought to myself at the time, *She's obviously hooked pretty good, so I can probably reach over and land her by hand.* But I then thought, *Okay, why take a chance? I'll let Don net her.* As I was leading her toward the net, I guess Don got a little excited when he saw how big she was, and he misjudged the distance between the smallmouth and the net. As he lifted the net to land her, the rim hit her broadside, and she was able to get just enough leverage to throw the hook and swim off. I was just sick about that one, because I so wanted a picture of the fish with me and my fly rod. But at least I had witnesses to the fish, and that helped somewhat, but man, would I have loved to have had some proof of my prize fish to take back home to show all my Oklahoma buddies.

This brings me back to my most recent lost fish that I mentioned earlier at the beginning of this chapter. It happened on a lake that I had just discovered, located about four miles from my house, Oklahoma Lake. It's a private lake, and the daily fee for fishing it is ten dollars. This was my second scouting trip in late October. It was a beautiful eighty-degree sunny day, but the wind was out of the south at twenty miles per hour, making it somewhat of a challenge to fish with a fly rod. I was in my Hobie Cat kick boat, and navigating it in the wind also proved challenging. A. B. was with me, and he wasn't having any luck at all. I wasn't doing much better, having landed a single bass that probably went about one and a half pounds. I had just switched to a very small segmented hard plastic bait made for use with a fly rod and called a KAWO Glide Swimbait, which looked identical to a small shiner swimming in the water. I flipped it out a few feet to test the action when this monster bass came from out of nowhere to drill it.

I only had about ten feet of line out, so I fed her more line to keep from getting broken off. I knew she was big, but had no idea she was in the monster class. I stuck the tip of my Scott 9½-foot 8-weight rod about three feet into the water to try and keep her from jumping, with the intent of lessening her ability to throw the hook. The bait I was using had a single, very small #12 treble hook attached to the belly, and I had a history of losing numerous fish with it by them throwing the lure when they jumped. Every jump of the fish with that particular lure was flirting with disaster. I wasn't about to let that happen to this fish. But I knew that at some point during the fight I was going to have to raise the tip of my rod out of the water to land her. After I thought I had her sufficiently worn out, and with my leader connection about to go through the tip-top of my rod, I felt as though I was ready to lip her and bring her in for a picture. That's when she made her only and final jump, and sure enough, she tossed the lure right at me. As Maxwell Smart would say, "I missed her by that much!"

After seeing her up close and personal, I could see she was every bit as big as I thought she might be, and she would have been my biggest bass to date on a fly rod. Oh, how that one still hurts! A. B. was not around, so once again there were no witnesses and no evidence other than the heartbroken look on my face when I saw him later. We had walkie talkies with us, and I got on the radio and exclaimed, "I just lost a huge bass." Of course, his first response was "What are you using?" Really big bass on a fly rod are difficult to come by, and at my age, this may have been that once-in-a-lifetime fish—a golfer's hole-in-one! Oh well, it just let me know how little I've progressed in sixty plus years of fishing toward becoming that self-actualized angler, but it's still an aspiration I have.

John Davenport, a noted fly-fisher in Colorado, has devised a system that might aid me somewhat in helping to ease the pain of a lost fish. He describes it in his book *Get Into Fly Fishing For Under $100*. John says you can count success with fly-fishing if you get a hit, a look, a rejection, a hook-up, a run, an in-stream release, a fish in hand, or a fish in the net. Specifically, his definition of success looks like this:

- If a fish has made a splash at the fly, it means you've had a good drift with the right fly in a place where there actually are fish. Congratulations! Count this as a hit.
- If you can see a fish follow your fly during your drift and then move away, you've had pretty good drift with

almost the right fly. This is good. Try again with a better drift, and after eight attempts, switch to another fly of the same type. Count this as a look or a rejection.

- If you felt a jiggle on your line or felt a pull and saw a flash near where you fly was drifting, you've had a hook-up. This is excellent. Your reaction time was just a little slow in tightening up the line by raising your rod. Count this as a hook-up.
- If the fish stays on for eight seconds (like bull-riding) you can count this as a catch. Say thank you as you quickly release it back into the stream. Kissing is done only in bass fishing.
- Size does *not* matter. Young fish are a sign of a healthy stream. Rejoice!

I would submit to you, fellow anglers, that Mr. Davenport is one of those rare self-actualized anglers. I'm not there yet, but I'm working on it.

Dr. Michelle Keylon, the deputy superintendent and chief operations officer at the Francis Tuttle Technology Center, who would succeed me as the superintendent when I retired, was often forced to listen to my fish stories when we would travel in the car together to attend professional meetings. After listening to one of my hard luck stories, she once asked me, "Why is it with you fishermen that the big ones always get away?"—with just a hint of incredulity in her voice. But she was always such a good listener, so I tried to be as academic as I could, listing every reason I could come up with, including how hard their mouths are (especially with bigger bass), thus making it difficult to set the hook, and just the sheer size and power of the fish, which gives it the opportunity to have its way with the fisherman and head for cover, leaving you helpless to do anything about it with light tackle. But those answers really didn't satisfy even me. I guess the real answer might lie in the fact that anglers are eternal optimists who assuage the hurt of loss with a spirit of hope that tomorrow we will best the prize fish we seek. Maybe just talking about the loss is good therapy!

CHAPTER 6

FISHERY HAREM

Learning a new lake, river, stream, or pond is a little like dating. At first you don't know a lot about the other person. Maybe you've asked a friend about your prospective match or done a little research on the person by googling his or her name on the internet, but until you begin dating, you never know what you're getting yourself into. Every fishery has a story to tell. Maybe it was created and raised in a near perfect environment and has all the right physical features. Maybe it was a victim of neglect or even abuse. Maybe it's unpredictable, unattractive, or even a psychopath. Just about any trait you can assign to a human being can probably also be assigned to a body of water that holds fish. But getting to know that body is part of the process, and it is typically an experience that can be both fun and frustrating. Fortunately, anglers don't have to be monogamous when it comes to the number of fisheries they can consider their own, and there are plenty of options to pursue during the courting process. But learning a new water is fun as long as you are patient and accept the fact that some fisheries can be learned fairly quickly while others may be an ongoing commitment that never seems to end. Which ones you prefer to spend most of your time on probably depends on your psychological makeup. But every angler has his or her own personal harem of places to fish, and as far as I'm concerned, the more the merrier.

This chapter will get into the fisheries that I've fished: those that I love, those that I hate, those I have love/hate relationships with, and those that I'd like to get to know better.

Three of My Harem Favorites (Lakes)

Sooner Lake, Red Rock, Oklahoma: This is the first impoundment that I can say I learned pretty well pretty quickly. While I was living in Stillwater, Oklahoma, I fished it often with good success most of the time. These were the days when I had a bass boat, and Sooner was only about a forty-five-minute drive from my house. It was always pretty clear by Oklahoma standards and was just a pleasant lake to be on. One of my favorite ways to fish it was to troll the riprap with a crank bait until I would get a hit and then anchor down and take some time to fish that area more thoroughly. I always enjoyed trolling Sooner because I never knew what I was going to get. I've caught bass as large as four pounds fishing this way, and my son Jim even caught a four-pound drum and a five-pound carp by trolling a crank bait.

Sooner was constructed as a source of cooling water for the Oklahoma Gas and Electric (OG&E) company's power plant. Because of this, it also provided wonderful winter fishing in those areas that were in close proximity to where the water exited the plant. While boats were not allowed in that part of the lake, shore fishermen could experience some of the best hybrid striper fishing anywhere in the state. In fact, my wife Cindy caught a 7 ½-pound hybrid on a fly rod in this area that literally left her fingers bleeding from the powerful runs it made. I bet next time she'll try harder to get it on the reel! I've also caught some nice walleye and largemouth in that area. January and February were always the best months for me to fish the plant water outlet area.

Sooner was built on a flat prairie, and the slightest amount of wind makes it unnavigable in a bass boat. There were many times that I trailered my boat to the lake only to head right back home because of rough water. What was a mild breeze at home in Stillwater turned into a gale on the high plains surrounding Sooner, and there was absolutely no cover anywhere on the lake that would protect me from the wind. But during my bass boat years, it was a favorite, and I rarely had an unproductive day of fishing there.

Hefner Lake, Oklahoma City, Oklahoma: This was my home water during the time I lived in northwest Oklahoma City. It was only about a fifteen-minute drive from my house and provided me with some of the most productive fishing using a fly rod that I could have ever have hoped for. I no longer had my bass boat during this time and was exclusively a fly-fisher, so I fished Hefner either from shore, by wading in the shallows, or from my Hobie Cat kick boat. Hefner is another lake constructed on the high prairie, and much like Sooner, the water can get angry very quickly. I was fishing the riprap along the dam in my kick boat one evening when the wind picked up, requiring me to row against it to get to my launch site. For a while I thought I was going to have to tie up my Hobie Cat and pick it up the next day. I didn't think I was ever going to make the half-mile trip back to where my vehicle was parked. After that experience, I began paying closer attention to the weather forecast on the days I planned to fish Hefner.

Cindy and I are members of the Oklahoma City Boat Club there, and one of my favorite spots to fish from shore is along the boat docks, in one of its few protected coves. Similar to Sooner, I've caught numerous species there, but these were all on a fly rod. This includes channel cats, walleyes, largemouth bass, crappies, bluegills, green sunfish, longear sunfish, bullheads, hybrid striped bass, drum, carp, gizzard shad, and even a flathead catfish. Lake Hefner has recently cleared up to be a pristine lake because of the unwelcome introduction of zebra mussels. The clear water is a nice byproduct of this invasive species. A side benefit of Hefner is having access to a string of three small ponds directly below the dam on the east side. It is here that I have experienced some of the best sight fishing for carp anywhere in the state.

Taylor Lake, Rush Springs, Oklahoma: Taylor is another wonderful reservoir for the fly-fisher and is the lake where I caught my first carp on a fly rod. A large portion of the lake is surrounded by cattails and water willows in about two to three feet of water, making it a great feeding area for carp. The bottom is hard-packed and easy to wade and sight fish for tailing carp. The lake is clear, making the carp easy to see. Of course, that also makes it easier for them to see you! I mostly wade this lake, but I have taken my kick boat there on occasion and been very successful catching largemouth bass and channel catfish. One of my favorite routines in fishing Taylor is to get up early enough during the summer months to make the hour drive in time to be on the water just as the sun comes up, launch my kick boat, fish for bass until it starts getting hot, and then load the boat back in the truck and wet wade for carp for the remainder of the day. The carp actually seem to enjoy the summer heat and start becoming active feeders about the same time the bass turn off. It makes for a great day of fishing for both species during the hot summer months.

Three of My Harem Favorites (Ponds)

Adolph Friedemann Pond, Payne County, Oklahoma: This is the larger of two ponds on my parents' farm, and one I grew up with, so I know it like the back of my hand. I was only nine years old when my dad first built it, and it was a pretty good bass pond even then. A few years later, Dad drained it and tripled its size. This was perfect timing, as I was just beginning to get into the science of farm pond management and could apply the knowledge I had acquired from my research to actual use in a real pond built from scratch. Before the rebuilt pond filled up, I went to the local tire store and strategically located three pickup loads of tires throughout the pond so that only I would know where some of the deeper man-made structures would be hidden when the pond filled up. This was a tremendous advantage especially during the summer and winter months, when the fish would head for deep water. My internal GPS still can locate these spots today, but with today's modern technology, if I were doing it now, I'd "ping" each location.

I personally stocked the pond with bass, crappie, bluegill, and redear sunfish from neighboring farm ponds. Then, to balance things out, I purchased some channel catfish from a commercial fish hatchery to put in the pond. Then, by a stroke of luck, I one day just happened to be strolling by Theta Pond on the campus of Oklahoma State University and noticed two students releasing some fish into the water. I engaged in some friendly conversation and discovered they were conducting some research as part of their wildlife management studies at OSU. I managed to persuade them to donate about three dozen fingerlings to transfer into Dad's pond and offered free access to it if they wanted to include that fishery in their research project. The neat thing about all of this was that the fish they were studying were orange spotted sunfish, which never get any bigger than four inches, making them ideal for serving as baitfish for bass, crappie, and channel cat. Additionally, I seined a good number of mosquitofish from a nearby creek and transferred them to the pond to assure a good self-sustaining population of baitfish. I also brought in from neighboring ponds my favorite vegetation to provide more habitat and help to keep the water clear. The result was as close to a perfect farm pond as I've ever had the occasion to fish.

For about the first twenty years of its existence, I restricted the fishing to only friends and family and strictly enforced keeping every bass under fourteen inches in length (they're the best eating anyway) and returning every fish to the water that was fourteen inches or over. Anglers could keep as many of the other species as they wanted with no size restrictions. The result was a well-managed pond that consistently produced big bass every month of the year at nearly any time of the day. This pond is simply amazing. My parents loved to eat fish, and I would frequently ask them whether they were ready for a meal of fish, and if the answer was yes, I would simply go out and catch a mess of twelve- to thirteen-inch fish for them to eat. It was nearly automatic any time of the year. I still love going out there and fishing it because catching big bass and huge bluegill never gets old.

Jantz Pond, Washita County, Oklahoma: This is the only pond I've ever fished that rivals my parents' pond in productivity. Jantz Pond is quite a bit bigger and has more structure. It looks as if it was a watershed lake that was built for flood control. I haven't fished it all that much, but it has the same characteristics as Dad's pond in terms of quality fish. I always catch big bass and huge bluegill every time I go out there. Dad's pond is always clear, but this one is gin clear, and you can see all the way to the bottom throughout the entire pond. There have been times when I have been rowing my Hobie Cat in search of a good spot to fish and have looked straight down and seen bass in the four- to six-pound range just casually swimming near the bottom for no apparent reason other than that they were just happy to be in such pristine water. I'm occasionally invited by Ron Jantz, who attends the same church I do, to fish this pond; and when Ron extends the invite, I clear my calendar so I can fish it with him. Because I see Ron at church every Sunday, I'm able to keep up with its success, and it appears that he also consistently catches big fish year-round. This is a special pond indeed!

Strate Pond, Garfield County, Oklahoma: Dr. Jim Strate is a very dear friend and was the superintendent of Autry Technology Center in Enid about the same time I was at Francis Tuttle. Jim and his wife Sharon have a cattle ranch near Covington, Oklahoma. Now that he is retired from Autry Tech, he is able to devote much more of his time to the family cattle operation. He tells me that the person he purchased the ranch from was a passionate bass fisherman and specifically built this pond for bass fishing with all the necessary habitat to sustain a healthy bass population. I mean, it has everything: a natural waterfall where a creek feeds water into the pond, strategically created islands, cozy necks, and shallow flats just perfect for spawning beds. It's obvious that the person who designed this pond took as much care in the detail as Arnold Palmer would in designing a premier golf course. And the fishing productivity shows the design was a great success. I look forward to fishing this pond every time I go with the same enthusiasm I have for fishing my Dad's pond. I have never failed to catch quality bass every time I've had the good fortune to be able to fish it.

Three of My Harem Favorites (Rivers)

Rio Grande, New Mexico (John Dunn Bridge): I get just as excited about fishing the Rio Grande in New Mexico as an Oklahoma weatherman does during tornado season. The steep and rocky descent to the river is no place for the family sedan, so you had better plan on taking a truck or SUV as you exit off Highway 522 and follow the Rio Hondo down to the Rio Grande. Once you've arrived, you have as much water as you have the energy to hike to, and there are nice holes all up and down the river. I usually fish it in the fall, after the white water rafters have left and the browns and rainbows are eager to get some pounds on before the onslaught of winter. There usually isn't a lot of fishing traffic, and even during the times there are, you can always hike away from them and find a productive hole that you have all to yourself. If you choose to explore the river and hike downriver and down the trail, I need to warn you that there is a natural hot spring not far from the riverbank that is frequented by both locals and tourists and evidently is a bathing-suit-optional area. So if you happen to come upon it, don't say I didn't warn you. Cindy and I went there one year with some friends (in our bathing suits) and had a great time enjoying one of God's wonderful gifts to that river.

Every type of pattern imaginable works throughout this stretch, but the most consistent producer is a simple black-and-yellow marabou jig. Additionally, my son Jim has created his own Rio Grande special that he's fooled some really nice browns with. It's basically a chain-head Woolly Bugger tied with brown hackle, brown marabou, and brown chenille. An added benefit of fishing this part of the Rio Grande is easy access to the Rio Hondo where it enters the Rio Grande right at the John Dunn bridge. The Hondo is a tiny stream, and the fish in it are much smaller than in the Rio Grande, but it has some great pocket water full of willing browns and rainbows who seem to prefer dry flies over anything else. So, for those rare times the Rio Grande isn't producing, you can always count on getting into plenty of action on the Rio Hondo, and nobody ever seems to fish it—at least I've never seen another angler on it during the times I've been there.

Lower Mountain Fork River, Oklahoma: This is a splendid fishery and the crown jewel of Oklahoma trout fishing. I particularly love the stretch of water below the reregulation dam. If you love mixed-bag fishing, this is your place. I've caught browns, rainbows, walleye, smallmouth bass, green sunfish, and hybrid stripers in that stretch. I'm convinced that if you were to put on some scuba gear and station yourself at the bottom, it would look similar to those freshwater aquariums you see at your local Bass Pro Shops and Cabela's. I can always count on catching something there, and many times it will be a strange warm-and-cold-water trifecta of some kind, such as a walleye, smallmouth, and rainbow.

Rio Costilla, New Mexico: This is great fishery for catching native wild cutthroats. When the water flow is good, there are usually plenty of fishermen there, but there are so many places to fish that you don't ever feel crowded. It's an hour drive from my cabin in Red River, and the last stretch of road is characterized by some of the roughest washboards you'll find anywhere on this continent. In fact, I lost a whole day of fishing one year because of a blown tire on that road. And they were brand-new tires! The biggest challenge with fishing the Rio Costilla, at least in the fall when we typically get out there, is having adequate water flow. As it is a tailwater, you always want to check in with the local fly shop before you make the commitment of tolerating the long, rough drive out there.

Three Lakes in Serious Danger of Having Our Dating Relationship Terminated

As with any courting process, there are times when you've had enough dates with a lake, river, or pond to tell you that this thing just isn't going to work out. For whatever reason, you can never seem to get into a fish-catching rhythm on such waters, and it is just best for everyone concerned to cut his or her losses and say, "I'm going to spend my time concentrating on another relationship." When the relationship comes to that point, we just need to follow the advice Paul Simon gives us in the lyrics of his 1975 hit song "50 Ways to Leave Your Lover." Sometimes you just need to "Make a new plan Stan … No need to discuss much … And get yourself free." Following are three lakes where I'm close to getting myself free.

Lake Overholser, Oklahoma City, Oklahoma: When I was teaching at Putnam City West High School, this lake was only a block away from the school. If I had wanted to, I could have easily walked down to fish it during the lunch period. But I didn't, because I fished it enough during the evenings and weekends to know it would have only added to the stress that a teacher often faces in day-to-day teaching. This is a lake I could never figure out even though I constantly heard of people catching hybrid striped bass there. It wasn't known for its largemouth bass fishing, but I thought, *Heck, I should be able to catch one now and again.* Never happened! Overholser was also noted for its channel cats, and I never caught one of those either the entire time I was teaching in Oklahoma City. In fact, I never caught a single fish of any kind the entire time I lived just minutes away from this lake.

Later, when I moved back to Oklahoma City to take an administrative position at Francis Tuttle, I tried the lake again, figuring I had about thirty years' more experience and that was bound to make a difference. By this time I had converted to fly-fishing, so maybe this was a fly-fishing lake. I had heard from my fly-fishing buddy Tom Adams, who was the manager of a local outfitter in OKC, that you could really find a lot of feeding carp on the north end, in the shallow flats among the many cattail patches growing in that part of the lake. I was thinking this may be just like Taylor Lake only much closer. Hooray! I couldn't wait to tell A. B. about what Tom had said, and we went the very next day to the Overholser flats. We waded for hours and hours in the shallow flats and never saw a single carp. So, my Overholser jinx continued even after a thirty-year absence from fishing it. This lake must really hate me!

Finally, on May 17, 2015, I broke the thirty-year Overholser drought with a scrappy thirteen-inch white bass caught from (of all things) a fishing dock! This was during a spring when we had record rainfall and all the lakes and ponds in the area were muddy and overflowing their normal banks—all except Overholser, for some reason. It was still relatively clear and had close to normal water levels. I had just purchased my first tenkara rig and was anxious to try it out somewhere. So why not Overholser? I wouldn't catch anything, but I wanted to get a feel for the rod and see what using a tenkara rig felt like. I decided to fish one of the fishing docks on the east side because the shorelines were all muddy and had flooded vegetation for me to deal with. There must have been at least a half dozen bait fishermen on the dock I selected who were fishing for crappie and catfish. I must have looked really strange to them carrying this weird-looking rig without a reel, telescoping the rod to its full twelve-foot length, and casting a fly among all the bait that was being offered to the local population of fish. Before I made my first cast, I asked all of them whether they were having any luck, to which they all responded no. I thought to myself, *A typical Overholser day*. I kind of excused my way in between two fishermen who looked as if they wouldn't take much offense, and on one the first casts—*bam!*—a nice white bass gave me everything I wanted on my limber rod with a four-pound-test tippet. Everybody standing on the dock was amazed at my good fortune. Rather than risk lifting the fish out of the water onto the dock, I led her down the ramp to the shore, where it wasn't so crowded and where there wouldn't be any risk of getting tangled up with all the fishing line and bobbers out there.

After a spirited fight, I landed her on the grassy shoreline. I then gave the fish to one of the nearby fishermen, who politely allowed me to Al Capone my way into a fishing spot on the crowded dock. I then said to myself, "This is why I love to fish, because you just never know." But most importantly, the Overholser losing streak had finally ended. Renewed in spirit and energized with newly acquired optimism, I went fishing two more times after that trip, again with zero luck, so I guess it was all just an accident—an anomaly. Some things are just never meant to be, and I guess Overholser will never be a candidate for my harem of fisheries.

Eagle Nest Lake, Eagle Nest, New Mexico: For years, as I would drive to my cabin in Red River, I was always taken by this beautiful-looking alpine lake nestled in the Moreno Valley of New Mexico. I can't tell you how many times I thought to myself, *Maybe I should include it on the agenda for the annual fall trip I make with four of my fly-fishing buddies?* Then one year I heard that somebody unlawfully put some northern pike in it and that they had quickly taken over the lake and were posing a severe threat to the existing trout and salmon population. In fact, the New Mexico Department of Game and Fish was so concerned about the situation that they made it illegal to throw any pike that were caught back into the lake. Man, this sounded too good to be true: no size or bag limits, pike so plentiful that you were required to keep every fish regardless of size. I loved catching pike on a fly rod in Canada, and they were also one of my favorite table fish. I told our group about it and asked whether they wanted to give it a try. They jumped all over it.

Jim and A. B. had never caught a pike before, and they were excited to have the opportunity to catch a fish that had a reputation of being one of the meanest, most ferocious freshwater fish this side of the Atlantic Ocean. So we added bass-size fly rods to our packing list and carved out a day to fish Eagle Nest in pursuit of pike and anything else the lake might have to offer. I had plenty of pike flies from all my trips to Canada and gave some of my favorites to Jim. As we attempted to wade the shoreline, we were surprised to see heavy vegetation for about twenty feet out from the shoreline, and we noticed that we were sinking up to our knees in the mud and muck while wading to open water, just as we might in many of the lakes in Oklahoma. That was totally unexpected and really disappointing. The lake was low, which added to the muddy shoreline issues we experienced.

The first year we tried the lake, there were only four fish caught. Jim and I both landed two nice yellow perch, perfect for eating, and we kept them. Jim did get his twenty-pound-test monofilament line cleanly bitten off by a pike, but that was the only evidence we saw the entire day of northerns in the lake. The yellow perch were a first for Jim, so that was pretty neat. I take blame for Jim getting bitten off, because in Canada we used heavy twenty-pound mono, and that prevented nearly all the bite-offs, but now I wish we would have packed some wire leaders. I guess I thought the action would be so fast and furious that a few bite-offs could be tolerated. I didn't realize that would be our only pike take of the day.

The next year we got a little smarter and went to the local fly shop in Eagle Nest and purchased some bite-proof wire leader and a few local favorite pike flies recommended by the local guides. This time my good friend Bob Verboon brought his kayak and I brought my belly boat to enhance our odds a little. Son Jim and Cousin A. B. once again fished the shoreline with waders. I made the mistake of bringing my sink-tip rig, which was a disaster for this lake because of all the heavy vegetation throughout the water at nearly all depths. Bob, a trout purist, stayed with his nymph rig and focused on trout. A. B. and I got skunked, but Bob did manage to catch a nice seventeen-inch rainbow from his kayak on a nymph, and Jim hooked into what many of us thought was a pike, at least for a while. Using a huge four-inch-long hot-pink pike fly with a twenty-pound-test wire leader, he caught a nineteen-inch rainbow that jumped several times before he landed her. But that was it—no pike or any evidence of any the entire day. Jim's rainbow broke all the rules. She hit a huge bait with a wire tippet. Weren't trout supposed to be leader shy? I'm still trying to figure out Eagle Nest Lake, but it may be a while before I can convince A. B. and Jim to return for another crack at a big pike The lure of trout is just too tempting to risk another day of lake fishing in the mud and muck of Eagle Nest. Heck, we can do that in Oklahoma!

Lake Watonga, Watonga, Oklahoma: Lake Watonga is part of Roman Nose State Park in western Oklahoma. It's a beautiful crystal-clear lake with plenty of bassy-looking structure that is supposed to have a healthy population of largemouth bass and channel cats. During the winter months, the Oklahoma Department of Wildlife Conversation stocks the lake with rainbow trout. In fact, the state record rainbow was held for a while by this lake—a ten-pound ten-ounce brute. The lake is only a one-and-a-half-hour drive from Oklahoma City, so it's probably my closest trout fishery. But I've never been able to figure out how to catch either winter trout or spring and summer bass. In fact, my performance at this lake is even worse than at Overholser. Translated, that means zero fish for me at Watonga. I don't know exactly what I'm doing wrong, but it just isn't a good match for me. I would suspect that some of the reason I struggle there is because it's located in a State Park and gets a lot fishing pressure. Clear-water lakes in western Oklahoma are rare, so people flock out there to surround themselves with the unique natural beauty so close to Oklahoma City. But being skunked on trout is really troubling. Here again, I think I have a logical reason for that as well. I've never felt comfortable fishing for trout in still water. I like moving water, where I can see my dry fly or strike indicator drift downstream. And while I've always had great success using streamers, which you might think would be ideal for trout in lakes, I have failed miserably at streamer fishing in Watonga.

The ultimate embarrassment came one day when I was fishing with my St. Paul's Lutheran Church buddies Kent

Wallace, Lyle Sharping, and Ron Jantz, who all use power bait fished just off the bottom. We always kid each other about the best way to catch fish. All three are regular attendees on our annual trip to Roaring River in southwest Missouri, and while they will try a fly rod for a time, they will usually resort to their spinning rigs to catch fish. I give them a hard time about "Bubba fishing" for trout, and they dish it back out to me because of my reluctance to use anything but a fly rod for any kind of fish. We're all the best of friends, so it's good-natured fun both ways, but most of the time I am able to outfish them with my fly rod.

Every Sunday at church, they would always tell me about all the trout they caught every week in Watonga. So, one Sunday, I popped off and kind of implied that I could probably outfish them on Watonga with my fly rod and asked whether I could come along. I knew they usually fished out of a boat and anchored it at a favorite spot off the dam to do their bait fishing. My strategy was to take my Hobie Cat and row close to where they were fishing and throw streamers. They knew where the fish hung out on that lake, so the hard part of locating them would already be taken care of. The rest would take care of itself because of my self-proclaimed "superior" skill and talent with the long rod—or so I thought it would.

We met at a convenience store, and I followed them to the lake in my truck. Once we got there, they motored their boat to their favorite spot, and I rowed my Hobie Cat nearby. After each one of the guys limited out using power bait, I had yet to get a single hit. I was wishing I had my sink-tip rig or even a full-sink line because I was pretty sure I just wasn't getting deep enough, but at any rate, they had the last laugh but were too classy to rub it in very much. I haven't been back to that lake ever since, but I'm still not done courting it, and I'm hopeful that one day I can add it to my fishery harem.

Two Lakes That Have Some Serious Potential (Fresh Meat!)

And then there's the fresh meat: lakes, ponds, and rivers where you've just started your relationship and are in the learning stage of whether or not you want them to be part of your harem. I'm currently working on two such situations now, as this book is being written.

Lake Arcadia, Edmond, Oklahoma: This lake is just a brisk walk from my house and has some interesting possibilities. Being located close to Edmond, it receives a great deal of fishing pressure, but it's so close that I am bound and determined to make it part of my fishing harem. It contains a species that I have never caught before and would dearly love to add to my wall of fame. The Oklahoma Department of Wildlife Conversation has stocked saugeyes in it, and I know very little about this species other than that it's a cross between a walleye (which I have caught numerous times) and a sauger (which I have never caught). To date I've been able to catch bass as large as eighteen inches, channel cats of similar size, numerous white bass and crappie, but no saugeye. That's a very small sample size, but so far, it's been somewhat encouraging. I'm still spending much of my time scouting different spots to fish but haven't been able to settle into a productive pattern as of yet. My goal is to fish it hard and often this year and see if it has the potential of a lake like Hefner, Taylor, or Sooner. It's not a very pretty lake, being mud-stained, and it has more shallow shoreline than I would prefer, but there are some secluded coves with flooded trees, so there is some decent habitat. I'm looking forward to giving it a real test in the months to come.

Oklahoma Lake, Jones, Oklahoma: This is another lake that is really close to my house, (about a ten-minute drive), and it is ideally suited to fishing with a kick boat. Although it's smaller than Arcadia, it's a much cleaner lake and has a hard sandy bottom. I fished it only twice last year, but I caught some nice bass each time and lost one that may have been a new personal record, so I'm really optimistic about spending more time on it and learning about it in greater detail.

I've found in years past that if I really want to do it right, it's very difficult to take on more than two new fisheries in the dating process at any one time, so unless I discover a new lake, pond, or river that looks just too good to pass up, I'll probably be spending most of this year fishing my old reliables and, at the same time, trying to make a few scouting trips to either Arcadia or Oklahoma to get to know them better.

Just like the familiar saying we've all heard so many times, "so many fish, so little time," I hope to have enough time this year to add both of these lakes to my harem. The neat thing about pursuing this type of harem is that even if you have favorites, nobody gets jealous or ends up having their pet rabbit boiled in a pot!

CHAPTER 7

MATCH THE PLUG

Earlier this spring, I was fishing—with great success—some riprap from shore with my fly rod in Lake Arcadia, and a twenty-foot bass boat with all the bells and whistles pulled up and fished a nearby point within shouting distance of where I was fishing. After about thirty minutes of unsuccessful fishing, one of them shouted to me, "Having any luck?"

I responded, "Yes sir! I was just drilling the crappie about an hour ago but they've slacked off some."

After a brief hesitation, he shouted back. "You hittin' 'em with that fly rod?."

To which I replied with supreme confidence, "Oh yeah!"

I then heard him say to his fishing buddy, "I guess we need to get us some fly rods!"

One of the most frequent concerns voiced to me from people who are contemplating the sport of fly-fishing, especially in the Midwest, is the lack of places there are to go fly-fishing. Some of the folks I talk to, automatically assuming fly rods are the exclusive domain of salmonoids, will typically ask, "But how many places around here can you fly-fish?" My response oftentimes is "Show me a flooded wagon rut and I'll fish it with a fly rod." Of course, anything that has gills, eats, and swims can be caught on a fly rod, and it's just a matter of properly educating them on the subject, which I eagerly do with some follow-up conversation. Bass fishermen are especially skeptical because they may have had great success in the past catching bass with any number of bass lures on the market today and just don't see how a fly-fisher can duplicate that success with flies. But of course, we can. And if there is one thing we've been taught as fly anglers from the beginning, it's learning how to match the hatch. Using that same time-tested strategy for catching trout, let's change a few words as we get into warm-water fishing and begin talking about mastering the concept of matching the plug.

James Heddon has been credited with the idea of creating bass plugs for the mass market. A passionate whittler and fisherman, one day he was sitting near a pond, whittling on a plug of wood. When he finished, he casually threw it in to the water only to see a giant bass savagely engulf it as if it were a frog or dying baitfish. He thought to himself, *Hey, I may be on to something here,* and soon after he became the Henry Ford of the fishing lure industry. The Lucky 13 lure that he would later begin to mass produce looked very similar to that tossed piece of whittled wood and soon became the fishing lure industry's Model T. Since then, lures of all shapes and sizes have been developed to imitate anything a fish might view as prey. Warm-water fly anglers can learn a great deal from our conventional angling brothers and sisters in their approach to catching fish on those familiar hard-bodied lures manufactured by the major companies. We just have to be a little creative in designing and tying our flies, since many of the patterns that are typically found in the fly shops and mail-order catalogs are not designed to imitate something that has a built-in wiggle. When I get what I feel is a dis from a dyed-in-the-wool Bubba bass fisherman who thinks fly-fishing is only for bluegill in small farm ponds or trout in streams, I will typically challenge him to a duel; him with his Bubba gear (spinning or baitcasting rigs) and me with my 8-weight fly rig, and we'll fish for bass at some neutral site and see who is the more productive fisherman. I'll do this only if I sense a condescending attitude on his part. I haven't had many such opportunities, or takers for that matter, but I'm always ready to show Bubba the power of the long rod.

I don't particularly enjoy these outings, because it means competition, and competition tends to take some of the joy away from why I like to fish in the first place; but if someone really hacks me off, I'll do it to defend the honor of fly-fishers everywhere. To date, I've won about as many of these challenges as I've lost, but my showing is usually good enough to shut them up for a while and at least earn from them some respect for fly-fishing. It's always fun to see their eyes grow big when they see some of the flies I come to do battle with. I think they are impressed by the sheer size of the patterns I'm planning to use, as they must have been expecting to see a variety of little poppers or woolly worms to compete with their big spinnerbaits and crankbaits.

I had an interesting experience several years ago with a guide I thought about hiring on Grand Lake in Oklahoma. He came highly recommended to me, and I gave him a call. Since I like to always get to know my guides before I hire them, I sought to have a conversation with him on the phone. I won't use his real name, because I don't want to steer any business away from him, since he probably knows his trade and more than likely is a decent guide, but just for the sake of this story, let's call him Bubba. I was going to attend a career-tech superintendents' conference with my very dear friend Brady McCollough, who is a very passionate bass fisherman.

We decided to hire a guide the day before on nearby Grand Lake o' the Cherokees, a.k.a. Grand Lake.

Now, Brady is highly skilled basser, and his rod and reel of choice is a spinning rig, although he will dabble from time to time with the fly rod, so there's still hope for him. The conversation with Bubba went something like this: He answered the phone with "Hello, Bubba's Guide Service."

I began my part of the conversation by saying, "Hello, this is Tom Friedemann, and I'm going to be attending a conference at the Shangri-la Lodge out there and would like to come a day early to do some bass fishing on Grand Lake with a friend."

Bubba responded, "How much have either of you boys fished so I kind of know what to expect?" I assumed this was a crude attempt on his part to assess the situation and qualify his two potential customers.

I told him, "We are really experienced bass fishermen and have been doing it since we were kids."

"Great, then I won't have to do a lot of nurse-maidin', if you know what I mean. I always prefer experienced clients. We'll catch a lot of big bass."

Then I got a little technical with him and asked, "Where are you finding them this time of the year?"

Sensing that I was going to be a pretty knowledgeable client, he got a little more technical back at me and said, "We'll be looking for suspended bass off the bluffs in about twenty foot of water using a jig and pig."

I responded, "That's great; I know just what I'm going to start throwing at them."

He followed up with, "Oh, so you guys will be bringing your own equipment then?"

I said, "Yes, my friend will probably be using spinning gear, and I'll be using a fly rod."

There was a big hesitation at this point. Finally I heard the response with a chuckle in his voice. "Fly rod? Are you kidding me? Son, these are big fish, and they're deep."

I responded, "That's great. Can't wait to get out on the water and give it a go."

After another long period of silence, and with a hint of anger topped off by a condescending tone, he said simply, "You won't catch nuttin'."

I immediately responded, "Hey, you get me on top of some fish and let me worry about that. I'll catch my share."

"Well, I ain't never had a guy fish with a fly rod before, and I'm tellin' ya, you won't catch nuttin'," he repeated, this time with emphasis.

I said, "Okay, I think you've told me what I need to know. I'll get back with my buddy and let you know what we decide."

He hung up without even saying "good bye," "thank you," or "kiss my ———!" Needless to say, I never returned the phone call to Bubba. But I do have some regrets, thinking that this was a golden opportunity to educate Bubba about the myths of fly-fishing. But I just couldn't bring myself to pay good money to spend an entire day on the water with someone with that kind of personality.

One of the joys of warm-water fly-fishing is devising ways to match the likes of the old, traditional, conventional hard body lures that were originally made by famous manufacturers like Heddon, Arbogast, Creek Chub, Helin, Bomber, Storm, and Cordell, just to mention a few. You have to think outside the box sometimes, and to the purists in the fly-fishing community, some of the approaches I'm about to discuss will seem like blasphemy. I get much of my inspiration for writing this chapter from a book authored by Jack Ellis titled *Bassin' with a Fly Rod.* Jack talks about a time many years ago, when he would use a small Helin Flatfish and it "was widely accepted by all but the snobbiest of dry-fly purists." But some would ask, "Is it truly fly-fishing?" Jack's response to that subjective question was to recommend just calling it fly-rodding instead, to which nobody could argue. Today he says he spends "a lot of time bassin' with a fly rod" as opposed to saying he's fly-fishing for bass. His thinking on that subject really helped me as a fly-fisher to justify taking some tools out of Bubba's big tackle box and devising schemes that mimic what a professional bass fisherman might use during a tournament.

So let's get out of our comfort zone as fly-fishers and go fly-rodding instead of fly-fishing. The very first bass I caught and logged back when I was fourteen years old was caught on something called a Martin Fly Plug. It was made of solid wood and had a disproportionately large glass eye embedded in it. Today, in good condition, they're selling for up to fifty-five dollars on eBay. I think I may have paid only eighty-five cents each for the two I still have. It has an action similar to that of the old familiar Heddon Lucky 13. The name Fly Plug, chosen by the maker, seems like an oxymoron, but it can easily be thrown with an ultralight spinning rig as well as with an 8-weight fly rod.

The first rainbow trout I caught, at about the same time, was caught on a Fly Rod Lazy Ike—another bass plug knock-off. And some of the largest largemouth bass I've ever caught using a fly rod were caught on a Fly Rod Hula Popper, very similar to the much larger bass models made by Arbogast. Most ultralight spinning lures can easily be cast with an 8- or 9-weight fly rod. So the line between ultralight spinning and heavy-duty fly-roddin' is a fine one. But what if you want to go big for the really big bass? A rule of thumb that I was always taught by my elders as I was learning how to fish was that you use big baits for big fish because small baits, more often than not, are preferred only by small fish, especially with warm-water species like bass, pike, and walleyes. And while there are times when fishing conditions merit going small for larger bass, more often than not, only big baits will work for big fish and tiny Martin Fly Plugs, ultralight Lazy Ikes, and miniature Hula Poppers just won't work if your goal is a trophy fish. The smaller versions of their big brothers are already at the maximum weight that a fly rod can handle, so to go bigger you have to get back to fly-fishing basics and tie your own patterns using feathers, hair, or synthetic materials to achieve the size you need and still keep the weight of the pattern down to what you can throw. Weight is the friend of the baitcasting and spin fisherman but the enemy of the fly-fisher. As a rule, the heavier the bass lure, the farther you can cast it. It's the exact opposite with fly-fishing. There are many synthetic materials on the market today that can be used to tie custom flies that look similar to the famous bass lures used by conventional anglers. Here are a few examples.

The Plastic Worm

There are many ways to imitate this old standby. My first big bass that I landed using a fly rod was caught on something that was designed to imitate a worm. It was a Hank Roberts Hair Worm made from rabbit fur. It came in a variety of colors and looked great in the water. The main problem with this pattern was how heavy it would get once it got saturated with water. I made my own versions of the Hair Worm up to six inches long and would tie them on to jig heads, which made them even heavier to cast once they got wet. But even with limited casting range they were really effective big bass producers. Nowadays you can find lighter worm imitations made with synthetics, with countless variations in diameters and colors. My favorite worm pattern on the market today that utilizes a version of this marvelous material is Rainy's Ultimate Worm, which comes already rigged "Texas Style." But if you want to tie your own worm, it doesn't get any simpler than going to www.feather-craft.com and ordering some Dragon Tails and simply attaching them in any length to any size hook or jig you prefer and throwing it into some bassy-looking water. In my opinion, Dragon Tails are the perfect solution to tying the perfect plastic worm imitation for bass fly-roddin'. You'll find them in a multitude of sizes and colors to match any soft plastic bait you'd see in Bubba's tackle box.

The Crankbait

I suspect that there's not an angler alive who hasn't put on an artificial lure and, with only a few feet of line past the end of his or her rod tip, tested it in the water before making that first cast to see how well it wiggled. It seems that somehow, we can best judge a fishing lure's ability to catch fish by how well it wiggles. The old, traditional billed lures like the well-known Wiggle Wart, Big O, River Runt, and Mirro-Lure paved the way for all the lures you see on the market today. Then there are the banana-shaped baits like the Lazy Ike and Flatfish, and lipless crankbaits like the Tru-Shad, Sonic, and Rat-L-Trap. All have a great wiggle that would put a belly dancer to shame. Now you are probably asking yourself, "How can you get a fly to wiggle?" Fortunately, there are several ways the fly-fisher can achieve the alluring bass-catching wiggle.

First, there are some excellent fly-fishing wiggle baits on the market today for those times when the fish are really wanting some wiggle in their prey. One that I've had some success with is the Wobble Bugger, which borrows from the same banana-type design of Lazy Ike and Flatfish. It's made primarily of foam and has a built-in wiggle bass oftentimes cannot resist. And then there's a series of patterns designed by Bob Popovics—the Pop Lips Pumpkinseed, Pop Lips Perch, and Pop Lips Shiner—which all have wiggles similar to the billed lures like the Big O and Wiggle Wart crankbaits. Bob achieves a lightweight bill by using clear silicone rubber formed to make a bill when hardened. It's an amazing piece of work and provides the same exact wiggle as the traditional hard-bodied billed bass plugs. Another similar pattern on the market is Betts' Bull-It Head Flashdancer. Its diving lip is made from a sheet of .010 Mylar. The flies from both Popovics and Betts require perfect balance and precision positioning of the lip or bill, which is a remarkable feat in itself and one that far exceeds my fly-tying capabilities, so I'm just happy to be able to buy both of them at the local fly shop or online. However, for those of you who like a challenge, you can purchase premade bills online from www.feather-craft.com. Look for Greg's Flylipps. There is one problem that I often have with all these patterns. When I make a cast, the pattern will sometimes land upside down, and then the cast is basically a wasted effort, as I have yet to find a consistent way to turn the lure right side up on the retrieve. When the upside-down situation happens, I've found it best to just quickly retrieve the bait to a point where I can make a roll cast and hope it lands right side up.

There's also a way you can convert any traditional streamer into a wiggle bait by adding a Wigglefin Action Disc. This is simply a piece of hard plastic formed into a disc that you thread in front of any traditional fly. Put one of these transparent action discs in front of your Woolly Bugger or Zonker and presto, you have a fly that wiggles! It's a simple way to create a wiggle in any pattern you already have, and I've found it to be just the answer when I can't get a hit on anything else. The only problem I have with action discs is their tendency to break if they hit even the smallest obstruction on either the forward or back casts. I have to be very careful to make sure my casts are always on the mark. I guess I should be grateful to the makers of this marvelous piece of technology, because when I'm fishing with an action disc, I become a more fundamentally sound fly-caster as I make every effort to keep it from hitting anything but the water.

The Buzzbait

When I was a spin fisherman, catching a bass on a buzzbait was one of the most exciting ways to fish. There is something about a buzzbait that seems to make a bass just explode as if it has anger management issues. I think it's exciting to witness this strange-looking thing coming at you as you're reeling it in and then all of a sudden it just explodes like a torpedo fired by an Allied submarine that detonated prematurely on its way to a German battleship during WWII. When I discovered the fly rod equivalent of the conventional bass angler's buzzbait, I was pleased beyond measure.

You can easily tie buzzbait imitations yourself, but there are several on the market that I've found that work really well. One is the Bolstad Sputter Minnow. Its body consists of hollow tubing coated with epoxy so it floats with a propellor spinner blade in front of the body. When retrieved, it leaves a spray just like a baitfish would when moving away from prime cover and into the jaws of a hungry bass. Another pattern that I was able to purchase years ago from a mail-order catalog called *The Bass Pond* out of Littleton, Colorado, which I don't think is in business anymore, is a pattern called a Buzz-Tail Pencil Fry Popper. This is just basically a foam popper with a spinner at the rear of the bait, directly in front of its tail feathers. It's not really designed for a constant retrieve, but when you pop it, it leaves a tantalizing water spray to go along with the chugging noise made by the cup-shaped popper head. This has been one of my favorite patterns for bass, but I can no longer find it on the market.

Another buzzbait option for the fly-rodder is Pat Ehler's Buzz-Ard, which has a large buzzing, spraying propellor in front of a torpedo-shaped body followed by a rubber skirt. And Heddon now offers a fly-rod version of its world-famous Torpedo that it calls a Teeny Torpedo and is an exact replica of its original design.

My nephew Dolph Prater, who lives in Casper, Wyoming, made me a pattern that looks identical to a Dahlberg Diver with a propellor in front of the head. Combine the spray of the propellor with the enticing floating-diving action of the Dahlberg and you've got another water-spraying type of bait that bass just go nuts over under certain conditions. It has produced for me on numerous occasions. This was Dolph's original design, and I have urged him to get a patent on it before someone else claims it. I already have a name for it: Dolph's Buzz Diver. I love this bait, and it's now a critical part of my topwater selection for bass when they're active on the surface.

The Jerkbait

Jerkbaits are another exciting way to fish for bass and one of the easiest plugs to match with a fly. Probably the best one on the market is the Dahlberg Diver. This fly has long been a standard pattern for bass and is one of my most consistent producers. I tend to fish Dahlbergs a little slower with more time between jerks than I usually did fishing some of my

previous jerkbait favorites, such as the Rapala and Rattlin'
Rogue, but maybe that's because I'm older now and not nearly
as impatient as I was in my twenties, thirties, and forties.

Another jerkbait imitation that is really easy to tie consists
of taking a sandable foam cylinder that you can cut to your
liking in many fashions. You can make it look like a bullet,
carve out a V to make it look like a Lucky 13, or even add a
lip to it and make it act like a Rogue in the water. For added
action, add a Dragon Tail or some marabou and you're all set.
Talk about a great jerkbait! I get excited just thinking about
throwing one of these puppies to some good-looking bass
cover.

The Spoon

The metal spoon in its various forms, such as the Johnson Silver
Minnow, Rex Spoon, and Dardevle Spoon, has been around for
ages and is still one of the most time-tested standbys on the
market today. Fly-fishing spoons are also available in fly shops
and online, but I usually have to go to the saltwater fly section
to find them. The pattern I like best is the Dupre Weedless
Spoonfly, which is designed primarily for tarpon. I've found
that when the bass are hitting Johnson Silver Minnows, they'll
also hit the Dupre Spoonfly. They are made of molded epoxy,
which makes them very lightweight while still providing the
necessary size to attract larger bass. These patterns are great
early-season producers especially when the water may be
stained from the frequently occurring spring rains.

But if you want to go small, miniature metal spoons can
be found at www.tenkarabum.com. These amazing little lures
are manufactured in Japan by Daiwa and come in a variety of

attractive colors. I've found them to be particularly effective when fished with a strike indicator.

The Deep-Running Bait

This is the category that takes just about every Bubba fisherman by surprise. "How in the world," they ask, "can you get a fly down deep?" They go on to say, "That line you're using floats, and you're not going to get even the heaviest jig down deep where the real lunkers are sometimes." Of course, the only fly-fishing they've probably ever seen was their grandpa throwing poppers to bluegill, and they noticed how all that pretty, brightly colored line just kind of floats there on top. But they don't know what fly-fishers know, and that is that not all lines are floating lines. Sinking-head lines, especially those designed by Jim Teeny, are really good at achieving the necessary depths for most deep-water bass, and they cast like a dream. And in those extreme cases where you really have to get even deeper, there are always full-sink lines you can use. The largest freshwater fish I ever caught was a thirty-nine-inch northern pike on a full-sink line, and I doubt I ever would have gotten my Whitlock's Deep Sheep down to the necessary depth using a floating line. Just as during the forward cast, where the fly follows the line in the air to achieve the appropriate casting distance, the fly will also follow the line to whatever depth the line chooses to reach in the water. You don't depend on the size of the bill or the weight of the sinker or jig to get the lure down deep. All the hard work of getting the pattern down deep is done by the fly line. This "fly-following-the-demands-of-the-line concept" is sometimes difficult to comprehend by my non-fly-fishing friends.

The Spinnerbait

Duplicating the traditional offset spinnerbait for the fly-rodder is probably the easiest of all match-the-plug challenges, but interestingly enough I haven't been able to find such a pattern on the market, so I've had to come up with my own patterns. There are a number of ways to do this. The easiest is to go to your local fishing store and purchase some offset spinners and then attach any type of jig or weighted streamer, and there you have it—the fly-fisher's version of Bubba's spinnerbait. Another way to imitate this tried-and-true producer is to use JB Weld to attach a snap and swivel on the hook and, after the weld dries, attach the desired blade to the snap and then tie your favorite pattern to the hook. The thing I like about using JB Weld is that the hardened material makes a lightweight head suitable for attaching eyes. I'm not sure adding eyes really increases the pattern's effectiveness, but I think it looks better; and the better I think it looks, the more likely I am to have confidence in it while I'm fishing. Fly-fishing, like any sport, is many times a function of having confidence, and I need all the confidence I can get from whatever source I can get it from.

Cousin A. B. uses a different method to tie these patterns, and his look much more professional than mine. He simply attaches the snap and swivel with thread, glues it in place, and then adds the desired feathers, fur, hair, or synthetic material to complete the fly. I usually tie mine with bucktail, flashabou, or a combination of both. Both styles seem to work equally well. Fly rod spinnerbaits are excellent producers and work the same way that traditional spinnerbaits work for Bubba when he's fishing his bass tournaments.

CHAPTER 8

BUCK, MEGAN, AND YELLOW LADY

Growing up on the family farm, I never really felt as though I clearly understood the concept of pets. Oh, we would always have dogs and cats on the farm, but they were more like staff than pets, and each had its assigned duties. The dog's job description focused on helping to herd cattle and assist in keeping varmints away from the chicken house. Cats were valuable for their innate hunting ability when it came to keeping the granaries free from mice and rats. "She's a good mouser," we would always say when we found one of them devouring a fat rat or mouse. The bottom line was that both cats and dogs had jobs to do, and both were expected to earn their keep. I would notice from time to time that when one of our cats or dogs would engage in some negative behavior around the farm—such as maybe developing a taste for chicken eggs—it suddenly disappeared. To this day, I'm not sure what ever happened to these animals, because when I asked my father about it, he would be very elusive about the whole matter. But I will tell you this: when it occurred, it always involved a low-performing dog or cat; and when they suddenly were gone, it certainly motivated me to improve my job performance around the farm.

We weren't very creative in giving our staff any names. We had a black dog. We called him "Blackie." We also had a brown dog. We called him "Brownie." Down the road on my uncle Bert's farm, they had a spotted dog. They called him "Spot." Are you beginning to get the picture here? I guess we were afraid that giving them fancy names like Gigi or Fifi might give the impression to others that they were like family to us, and they clearly were not.

When I became an adult, I got a little more sophisticated in name selection, but—by force of habit, I guess—kind of followed that same pattern when it came to assigning names. When I had the opportunity to build our family's dream home on my parents' farm and had plenty of open land where a dog could roam free, we named our first canine pet there "Butterscotch" because she was that color. An Irish Setter came later that we named "Brick" because he was that color. And finally, we named a Golden Retriever "Buck" because of his buckskin coloring. We also had a big striped domestic cat we called "Yellow Lady" because of her yellow fur. We continued to evolve with assigning names and eventually became so bold as to give two of our Irish Setters human-like names: Megan and Jake. One thing I learned during this time was that it is easier to develop a deep personal relationship with animals once you don't view them as staff with assigned jobs to do. Once that stigma was removed, it became more likely for me to view them as family and come to appreciate their unique personalities that were able to grab huge parts of my heart.

Yellow Lady, for example, would always climb the huge pecan tree that overlooked our house and found one particular branch each morning where she could relax and stare at us through the skylight widow in our bedroom before she began her day. It was as if she couldn't begin her day until we woke up and began ours, so she would just patiently lie there waiting for us to get out of bed and acknowledge her by saying through the window, "Good morning, Yellow Lady." Unless she was on one of her weeklong hunts, she was always there to say good morning.

Often, following her hunts, she would bring back some game to lay at our front doorstep until we saw it and gave her proper due. "Good job, Yellow Lady. Way to go, Yellow Lady. Look at that big rat you killed. You are such a good cat," we would always say. Only after she was sufficiently complimented would she begin to eat it. Sometimes rigor mortis would set in if we weren't at home or were out of town for a few days, but she would never waste her kill and would always wind up eating every bit—bones, fur, and all. Yellow Lady was quite a hunter and, in addition to rats, would bring back squirrels and rabbits nearly as big as she was. Sometimes she came back from her hunts looking battered and bruised. There was no telling what kind of scraps she had gotten herself into, but after a few days of R and R and a whole lot of love from the family, she'd be off again on yet another hunting expedition. I've always heard that if you don't like cats, you haven't met the right one yet. Well, I was never particularly fond of cats until I met Yellow Lady.

In addition to this beloved cat, we also had two very special dogs that had a very special place in my heart—Buck and Megan. Buck, a Golden Retriever, loved to go fishing, while Megan, an Irish Setter, had a strong preference for hunting. Both had the same passion for their preferred sport as the most fanatical among us.

Buck would always get so excited the moment he saw me leave our house with my fly rod because he knew exactly what was getting ready to happen. It was just one hundred yards or so from my house to my parents' farm pond, and Buck would jump on me constantly with every step, barking the entire time with unbounded excitement until we got there. Sometimes I was so scratched up from the marks he made on my arms and legs with his happy paws that I was almost too injured to fish! When I got to a place along the shore where I wanted to fish, he would park himself right next to my right leg, occasionally leaning on it with the weight of his body. He would often lean on my leg so hard that I would nearly lose my balance while attempting to make a cast. I guess that was his way of showing his support. From there he would intently watch every cast I made. He especially liked it when I would use a popper, because he could visually follow each retrieve.

After a while, if he thought I was making too many casts without producing a strike, he would bark at me. Great! Just what I needed—added pressure from a four-legged critic. I was never sure whether those barks were words of encouragement, criticism, or advice, but there were times I wanted to throw the rod at him and say, "Okay buddy, let's see if you can do any better." It sure would have been nice to have known how to speak golden retriever back then.

When I finally got a fish on, Buck would go ballistic on me and soon show me why his breed had "retriever" in its name. He would charge into the water, evidently thinking it was his job now to retrieve the thing before it got off—another obvious recognition on his part that I lacked the necessary skills to do job all by myself. My remedy for this somewhat annoying bit of enthusiasm was to try to catch a small sunfish early and give it to him to maul. The fish would act as a chew toy and keep him occupied for an hour or two or until he wanted to fish again, but at least it bought me some uninterrupted time to dedicate to my fishing. He never ate the doggone things, and they didn't look very pretty after he was finished with them, but their carcasses provided an excellent meal for the racoons or crows that would come later to benefit from his sport. I never could convince Buck that fishing was not a team sport. He thought my job was to hook them and his job was to retrieve them, but at the end of the day, I guess I loved having a pet who was as passionate about fishing as I was.

I was never into hunting as much as fishing, but Megan, our female Irish Setter, never held that against me. Megan too, never quite understood what her role in hunting was. We got her because we loved the personalities of Irish Setters, not for their reputation as hunting dogs, but I guess she felt obliged to let me know that her breed had evolved for that purpose. I always loved combining dove hunting with fishing at a pond. I'd take my twelve-gauge shotgun and fly rod to the pond and fish until the doves would begin to fly in toward evening to water. Megan, with no apparent interest in fishing, knew when she saw my shotgun that hunting was somewhere on the agenda, so she just patiently sat by my side and watched me fish. When the doves started coming in, I would put down the fly rod, and hide under the willow trees, and begin firing away as they flew in. The first time I hunted with her, I thought this would be a neat deal, especially if one landed in the water. Megan could jump in and retrieve them, right? Wrong! I soon learned that she had more selfish motives. I shot three doves that first day with her, and she promptly ate every one of them. I'm sure a skilled dog trainer could have fixed the problem, but she was, after all, a family pet first, and I didn't hunt all that much anyway, so I just enjoyed our relationship for what it was. I shot and she ate. But there were times when I would beat her to a dove, and in that way, we had some friendly competition of who could get to the bird first; this just kind of added to the sport. I would shoot the dove and then race with

Megan to fetch it. I may have invented something—aerobic hunting?

Megan had some other endearing features to her personality. Irish Setters are such social creatures and when my wife and I would leave for work and the kids went off to school, she'd get very lonely. In our absence, much of her time was spent chasing cattle, much to the disdain of some local farmers, and one day she came back with a load of buckshot in her behind that required a visit to a veterinarian. She learned from that experience but unfortunately turned her interest to my dad's chickens, which were fenced up across the creek from our house about a half mile away on Dad's farm. One day Dad came to my house and said, "You're going to have to get rid of that red dog. She's been eating my chickens, and I caught her red-handed walking across the field with a chicken in her mouth while I was plowing that wheat field between our houses." He went on to say that when he went home, he found a big hole dug under the fence surrounding the chicken house and he was missing six of his best chickens.

Now remember what I said earlier in this chapter about how dogs would suddenly disappear on the farm when I was growing up because they had demonstrated undesirable behavior? Well, eating chickens is about as undesirable as egg sucking, and both crimes were certainly worthy of severe punishment or for eligibility in a relocation program somewhere. I knew I was going to have to give her away to a good home, and my wife and kids were all just sick about it. We all loved Megan, But I knew how much she loved eating doves and assumed that chickens had now taken their place on her menu.

But alas, just like a good whodunit on TV, not all the evidence was in yet. Several days later, as I was still trying to find a good home for Megan (Irish Setters who are used to roaming around free are not all that easy to give away), I got a knock on the door, and it was Dad. He started out by saying, "I need to apologize about Megan. I had her all wrong." It turned out that all six chickens were alive and well and living under a cedar tree just outside our house in a nearby pasture. Dad said he was plowing another field on the other side of our house and noticed something that looked like snow under one of the cedar trees. His curiosity got the best of him, and he got off the tractor for a closer inspection and saw Megan lying down with all six chickens. They were just sitting there, too scared to move. Dad said Megan looked happy and content staring at her six new best friends, but the chickens looked like six ivory statues petrified with fear. Dad then went home and got a portable pen and went to the tree and put all six chickens in the pen and returned them to the chicken yard. He said Megan just watched with her big, sad eyes, wondering why she couldn't have some friends while her human family was off to work and school. The chickens were all fine, although Dad said they didn't lay any eggs for over a month after their ordeal.

Now just stop and think about the lengths that Megan went to in transporting those six chickens to the location she had picked out for their playground. First, she had to dig a hole under the fence. Then she had to chase each one down without harming it, which couldn't have been easy. Then she had to, one at a time, carry the chickens carefully in her mouth so she wouldn't injure them during the half-mile journey across a creek and over a plowed field to the cedar tree near her doghouse! Now that's a real need to socialize with another living creature. After that, her human family paid a lot more attention to her, and she never did it again, and Dad became big a fan of hers from that point on. I think Megan convinced Dad to change his opinion a little bit about dogs being nothing more than staff on the farm. They have feelings too.

CHAPTER 9

FISHIN' BOATS

I owned my first boat when I was fourteen years old. It was a six-foot toy boat constructed of rigid plastic. I purchased it at the local TG&Y store in Stillwater. I'm sure it was designed for playing around in a swimming pool, but it made a wonderful fishing craft for the local farm ponds I fished. I got the idea from an older cousin, Paul Bamberger, who had an identical one he used to fish the ponds around his parents' farm in Perry, Oklahoma. It wasn't very stable, and I can remember having to carefully position myself in the center of the boat and sit cross-legged, similar to how you see people in Japan sit at their dinner tables. That was the only way I could stabilize the boat and keep it balanced. It looked like a miniature dinghy that you might see as a secondary watercraft to larger boats on larger bodies of water. I used a small wooden oar to propel myself to fishing spots on some of the larger ponds I fished that I could have never reached from shore. I had no life vest and could barely swim, but that didn't keep me from pursuing those spots I had always wanted to fish. I'm still in disbelief that my parents allowed me to purchase the boat and use it on the water. Maybe they didn't know what I was doing with it. At any rate, I was able to use it for only two seasons, as it began to crack from degradation caused by the sun and lack of proper storage during the winter months. But the thrill of hunting for fishing spots on the water and catching fish from a boat was addictive. As a result, I've owned some form of watercraft to fish with ever since.

The second boat I remember was a joint venture with my cousin A. B. Together we purchased a two-man inflatable rubber raft and kept it stored in his parents' garage. It served its purpose well and was far safer than my plastic toy boat, which would have sunk like a rock if I had ever capsized in it. That was the first time I fished with A. B. in a boat—an experience we were able to repeat later as adults when we both purchased bass boats.

But what was really the ultimate in-the-water experience was when we both purchased tube floaters to really get out among them. My first tube float was one made of canvas material and manufactured locally in Oklahoma City, on Portland Avenue, by Fishmaster. The first ones put out by Fishmaster were pretty crude, and you had to supply your own inner tube to put inside the floater. That was no problem for me; Dad always seemed to have a tractor tire inner tube that was no longer functional for farm work but with a few Camel vulcanized patches was perfect for my Fishmaster tube.

Fishmaster also sold some uniquely designed boot fins they called paddle pushers that were made to be affixed to wading boots. As one made an easy walking motion while comfortably seated in the Fishmaster, these ingenious inventions would propel the wearer forward rather than backward (the direction traditional swim fins send float tube users). To this day I prefer the paddle pushers to fins because I can maneuver myself into a better fishing position facing my targeted destination while moving forward instead of backward. The only problems I had with inner tube floaters were that they sat very low in the water, giving me a poor view of my surroundings, and there was always the issue of whether or not I had enough air in the tube to keep it safe and navigable. Maybe if I hadn't been using Dad's old, worn-out inner tubes, the latter would not have been a problem. I can't remember ever buying a new inner tube for my Fishmaster. When I needed to replace a tube that was beyond repair, I would just ask Dad whether he had a tube I could use, and he always seemed to find one for me.

I discovered a solution to the inflatable tube problem when I located a hard polymer belly boat at the local Gibson's Discount Center. This hard-body floater had custom-made indentions where I could install three standard-size plastic tackle boxes. The old Fishmaster had a sewn-in canvas compartment located on top of the tube where I could store a few small tackle boxes, but it always left something to be desired in terms of the amount of gear I could take with me on the water. Additionally, the new belly boat had another smaller but deeper indention where I could insert the rod butt of an extra rod. And I particularly enjoyed the form-fitted seat with a high chair back that provided much greater comfort than the Fishmaster canvas seat that would always ride up on me after a few minutes of being suspended in the water. This always resulted in an extremely uncomfortable wedgie! Most importantly, the hard-bodied version was designed for the user to sit high in the water, giving me a much better view of my surroundings.

I loved my new polymer floater, and I literally wore it out after many years of heavy use. Eventually it began to develop hairline cracks and started to take on water to the point that it would list from one side to the other. All my attempts to patch it were unsuccessful, so I had to find a replacement, which turned out to be quite a challenge.

Evidently the rest of the fishermen out there are not as enamored with hard-bodied tube floats as I am, because all I can find in Bass Pro Shops or Academy Sports and Outdoors, or even from eBay or Amazon, are the inflatable versions. I'm not sure I understand all that, but to each his own, I guess. After an exhaustive search, I finally found one at the Zebco Outlet Store in Stroud, Oklahoma, and bought it without hesitation. This hard-bodied vessel was made by Browning, and they called it their "Laker" model. It is U-shaped, which makes it better suited for going backward than forward, which would mean it was probably designed for use with fins rather than paddle pushers, but that was something I could live with because it had everything else I wanted in a belly boat. I purchased some swim fins with the idea that I would now probably be traveling backward more than forward, and off I went to the water. I loved my new Laker even more than my previous belly boat, which I didn't think was possible. I was able to propel it better with the pushers than I had hoped, and it seemed to sit even higher in the water, which was a sheer delight. One feature I particularly liked about it was that it appeared to be designed for fly-fishers. Since it was U-shaped, it had a snap-on apron that went across the open part of the U and served as a nice stripping area for my fly line. There is a picture of it with me in it on the back cover of my first book, and I'm still using it today.

Of course, there was also the bass boat stage in my life, which covered a period from 1976 through 2000. With a young family by this time, we purchased something that could be used for both pleasure boating as well as serious fishing. The affordable boat of choice was a fourteen-foot Terry Sportsman tri-hull with a forty-horsepower Evinrude outboard motor. Terry bass boats were manufactured in Louisiana by the Terry/Delhi Manufacturing Company and were the number two sales leader among bass boats in the nation at the time, surpassed only by Forest Wood's Ranger bass boats. So I was very proud to have one, even though it was at the bottom of the line in their product offering; it was kind of like buying a base Mercedes with no frills. Surprisingly, it had sufficient power to get a slalom skier out of the water, and we used it nearly every weekend for either family entertainment or bass fishing. It was tan with bright orange seats and orange accessories.

Two years later, we purchased a tan 1978 GMC VanDura and had it customized with orange accents. The van and boat were a perfect match with each other, and my family was so proud to pull it to lakes all over Oklahoma and Missouri. Because it was a compromise gift for the family designed for both fishing and pleasure boating, I always carried a spinning rod and reel in one of the compartments and jokingly warned my kids that if I was ever pulling one of them on skis and saw some surface activity, I would stop the boat that instant and begin fishing. I think they thought I was just kidding, and maybe I was at the time I said it, but the temptation was just too much to resist one sunny afternoon.

I was pulling my daughter Kari on a beautiful wind-still day on Lake Carl Blackwell, west of Stillwater, when I could see I that was headed straight toward a school of boiling sandies (white bass) aggressively feeding. Without thinking, I immediately shut the engine down, retrieved my stored spinning rig, and began hauling in one fish after another as they were just drilling my white lipless crankbait. While this was happening, Kari slowly descended into the water and screamed back at us, "What happened? Why'd you stop?" Jo, my first wife, yelled back at her, "Your dad found a school of feeding fish, and he's going to fish for a while until they quit. Just hold up your ski to let any other boaters know where you are, and we'll be watching out for them too. It shouldn't be too long."

These opportunities are just too good to pass up, and of course it didn't last very long, but we had our supper for that evening. I started the boat back up and resumed pulling Kari around the lake, but she loves to tell that story. I told her later that when your dad is a passionate fisherman, sometimes you have to make adjustments. After all, didn't she like having fresh fish for supper?

That boat served as some relatively cheap recreation every summer, as we had a group of friends who also had boats and we would meet nearly every weekend at some lake to either fish or water-ski. In all, there were six families that totaled two bass boats, three ski boats, and one pontoon party boat. One of the families, Jim and Paula Short, also had a mobile home on the shores of Tenkiller Lake, and we would spend many weekends there as well. It was a fun time for us and our kids, and it created a special bond among the six families, as well as a genuine love for the water.

When I converted to fly-fishing and Jim and Kari left the nest to begin families of their own, the bass boat got used less and less, and I decided to sell it. That was a very sad day for me. It never gave me any trouble the entire twenty-four years I owned it, and I loved taking it out on the lake and fishing in it, but the time had come to either replace it or move on to a watercraft more suitable to my rediscovered passion, fly-fishing.

I recall reading an article in a fly-fishing magazine that featured a fly angler fishing from a kick boat. Wow! It looked like a fun, comfortable way to fly-fish in the water. Again, just like tube floaters, nearly all the kick boats you find on the market are inflatable, and I wasn't interested in that. But Cabela's did have a single hard-body kick boat made by Hobie, and it seemed perfect for my type of fishing. Officially it was called a Hobie Float Cat 75 Pontoon Kick Boat, but I call it a Hobie Cat for short. I ordered it, and it arrived at my house a few days later unassembled. As I recall, it took me nearly half a day to put it all together. I couldn't wait to get it out on the water for a field test. By this time, I was single and living on Eagle Lake in Oklahoma City so I only had to go to my backyard dock to launch it. I couldn't believe how comfortable it was to fish from. The oars allowed me to go either forward or backward, allowing me to get to a fishing spot twice as fast as I could in my Browning Laker floater. When I wasn't fishing, I could put my feet on the footrests and it was like fishing from the family La-Z-Boy Recliner. It is still my favorite fishing craft today, and I've used it on huge lakes in Oklahoma as well as small farm ponds. It is the perfect fit for me.

The author in his floating La-Z-Boy fishing chair (a.k.a. Hobie Cat Kick Boat).

While living on Eagle Lake, I also purchased a Pelican Paddle Boat, primarily to take the grandkids for a boat ride when they came to visit, since it comfortably held four passengers. But to my pleasant surprise, it also made a very efficient fishing rig. It was especially good for trolling, which I often did just to locate bass in this lake that I was unfamiliar with. I would often get in it and troll up and down the lake with my fly rod and a full-sink line to search for bass, and I was extremely successful at it. Once I found a productive spot, I would make a note of it and return with my Hobie Cat to fish it a little more seriously. I especially enjoyed using the paddle boat to troll during the dog days of summer with the temperatures approaching one hundred degrees. During those times, I would troll over the deepest part of the lake near the dam so see if there were any big bass lurking around some hidden structure that I wasn't aware of, and many times I accidently hooked up with either a big bass or channel cat. I called it aerobic fishing, since I was getting in some good exercise with the constant pedaling. It was just like using a stationary exercise bike at the gym, only I had a good chance of catching a fish. How great is that?

When Cindy and I married and moved to another house on yet another lake, Blue Stem, I purchased a johnboat for use on that impoundment similar to what I had used the Pelican Paddle boat for. I bought a twelve-foot Tracker model from Bass Pro and matched it up with a Minn Kota Endura 50 trolling motor with fifty pounds of thrust. A. B and I had a lot of fun fishing from it on Blue Stem Lake, but I was caught a little off-guard by its instability in the water. It kind of reminded me of that little blue plastic boat that I had bought years prior as a fourteen-year-old. I had to be careful, especially in rough water and when loading and unloading. But it served its purpose well, and the little trolling motor could really move two people around the lake all day on a single battery charge. I wouldn't change those times fishing together with A. B. for the world. The water belongs to the fish, but a boat allows us, as anglers, to get a little closer to their world and experience some of the joy they must have swimming free from shore to shore. In the 1964 motion picture *The Incredible Mr. Limpet*, Don Knotts plays the role of Henry Limpet, who partway through the film is transformed into an animated talking-fish character. A line I love from that movie that I often think about as I'm on the water looking down into the depths from my Hobie Cat, is when Henry, a shy, fish-loving bookkeeper, looks into the water and exclaims, "It must be wonderful down there in your world." The hard part is catching them and bringing them, if only temporarily, into our world.

CHAPTER 10

FISHIN' TRUCKS

I can't exactly remember the day I learned to drive; I only know it was a few years before I turned the legal driving age of sixteen. When you grow up on a farm, you begin driving about the same time you're tall enough to reach the clutch pedal of a pickup truck. During wheat harvest, I would drive either one of my dad's or one of my uncle's pickup trucks out in the field, following the combine until the hopper was full, and then carefully align the bed under the combine auger for unloading. It took about a hopper and a half to fill a half-ton pickup truck, and once it was fully loaded, I would meet one of my uncles on the country road where it intersected with the highway and exchange it for the empty truck they had just taken to the Stillwater Milling Company, where we sold our wheat. Of course, I was never allowed to drive underage on the highway, just on country roads and in the fields, following the combine driven by my dad. This went on every day, all day, until each field was cut and all the wheat safely stored in the grain elevator. So I got to drive my dad's pickup to local fishing ponds even before I was sixteen, as long as I was able to stay on country dirt roads. This wasn't too much of a legal stretch, since every pond I fished was just a few miles away from our farm.

Needless to say, I feel very sentimental about pickup trucks, and for nearly my entire life, I've always owned one or had access to one. Since I didn't grow up to be a farmer, I now use my pickup trucks primarily for fishing. To me, and I would suspect for most fishermen, a truck is something one develops a personal relationship with that is maybe similar to that of a cowboy and his horse. A truck can get you through some tough times and always come through for you.

My first fishin' truck was a red 1949 Dodge pickup. It was the one I learned to drive when I was a boy and later inherited as a young adult. It had a three-speed manual transmission with a stick on the floor and an ignition button also on the floor, next to the gas pedal. After it had outlived most of its usefulness on the farm, my dad bought a new truck for his primary farm vehicle and the older model became a second truck. As a backup truck, its duties were relegated primarily to hauling trash and transporting chicken manure. When the chicken house needed cleaning, we would always unload the nitrogen-rich animal by-product on an alkaline area of one of the wheat fields. It made great fertilizer. Nothing ever went to waste on a German farm!

My former father-in-law, Dr. Gene Acuff, was a sociology professor and department head at Oklahoma State University. He always wanted to farm and raise cattle, so he purchased a small acreage east of my parents' farm and persuaded my dad to sell him the old truck for the light duty it would see hauling feed to his cattle and occasionally pulling a stock trailer. When Gene later upgraded to a newer truck, he gave the old Dodge to me, which was a gift that I will always treasure. Oh, the memories I had of fishing with it as a young boy with my cousin A. B., and now I was reconnected to it as a young man just beginning his career. We were both nearly the same age; I was born in 1948, and it was manufactured in 1949, so it was almost like being rejoined with a twin brother. I had it fifteen years, and it followed me to my first job as the marketing education teacher at Putnam City West High School in Oklahoma City, then back to Stillwater when I joined the Oklahoma Department of Career-Tech Education, then to Cache in southwestern Oklahoma when I got my first administrator's job at the Great Plains Technology Center in Lawton, and then, finally, back to Stillwater when I rejoined the state career-tech department.

It seems I've had an experience for the ages with all my fishing trucks, and the one that sticks out the most is from when we were living in Cache, just across the road from the Wichita Mountains Wildlife Refuge. I had been fishing one summer evening at a farm pond near Indiahoma, and on the way back I thought I would stop for gas at the local quick-stop convenience store in Cache, about a mile from our house. It was dark as I pulled the truck next to a gas pump. Now, I loved my old Dodge pickup truck dearly, but sometimes when it would get really hot after a long trip like the one to Indiahoma I had just returned from, it wouldn't start after I turned off the ignition. It didn't always do it, which kept me from taking it to the shop for repair. Well, after the twenty-minute drive that evening, it decided it would pull one of those stunts, and I couldn't get it started after I had filled it up with gas. Of course, I knew exactly what to do. I would just let it sit for about ten to fifteen minutes and try it again, which never failed. While I was in the store, I thought I might as well get a beer and drink it outside for the required fifteen-minute wait. I told the clerk in the store what I was doing so he would understand why there was a vehicle taking up a filling station slot.

It was a quiet night in Cache, Oklahoma; there was not much going on except for some busy moths circling the gas station lights and the occasional coyote calling across the prairie, so I don't think the station lost any business during that fifteen-minute wait. After sufficient time had passed, I got inside the truck, and sure enough, it started up with no problems. As soon as I pulled on to the street, I immediately heard two sirens blaring and saw red and blue lights flashing in full display. These guys were after me and were riding my bumper like there was no tomorrow.

I immediately pulled over and heard one of the officers yell at me, "Get out of the truck with your hands up in the air and place them on the hood of the vehicle." They were obviously in no mood for any pleasant discussion, as they both had their service revolvers pulled and pointed straight at me. Of course I immediately responded, "What's this all about?" to which one of them replied, "Just shut up and do as I say!" So there I was, spread-eagle up against the truck, with one officer pointing his pistol at me while the other one was calling in to the station and saying, "I think we got him!"

I thought to myself, *Got who and for what?* They then searched my trusted friend, the old Dodge pickup truck, which must have been thinking to itself at the time, *I've never seen this guy before in my entire life.* Then, in an instant flash of self-reflection, I got to thinking about anything I had ever done that might have been against the law, and except for occasionally speeding or rolling a stop sign now and again, I came up totally empty. I never cheated on my taxes, never faulted on any debts to anybody, or even tore off one of those tags on my bed mattress. Heck, as a sales clerk at Katz Department Store, I had even helped an elderly lady cross a busy street at the intersection of Seventh and Main in bustling downtown Stillwater. What did they have on me? Then I thought to myself, *Is this all about the single can of Coors I consumed while waiting for the pickup to cool down? I mean, wow, isn't that a little harsh?* I was only a mile away for home, for crying out loud, and beer sold in convenience stores in Oklahoma at the time only had a 3.2 percent alcohol content anyway.

In the meantime, cars were going by very slowly, with everyone rubbernecking to see who was getting ready to go to jail. Cache, Oklahoma, is probably about the same size as Mayberry, North Carolina, and you can imagine what the townspeople in that small town might think if Andy and Barney had someone pulled over at gunpoint and spread eagle across the hood of a pickup truck in their community. This was a big deal in Cache! Also going through my head was the fact that I was the assistant superintendent at a nearby career-tech school in Lawton, and my wife at the time was a teacher at the local public school. I could see the headlines now: "Local School Administrator Arrested in Cache for [whatever it was that I had done]." My wife and kids would all be ashamed to go to school the next day. My career in public education was over. For what seemed like an eternity, I stood there, afraid to speak with a gun pointed at me while the other officer checked things out. Then the officer pointing the gun at me all of a sudden holstered his weapon and in a completely different tone of voice, calmly said, "Mr. Friedemann, we apologize, but there was a home invasion just west of here, and an elderly couple were tied up, beaten, and robbed at gunpoint. All we had to go on was a general description of the getaway vehicle, which was an old red pickup truck. We saw you pull into the convenience store thinking you were going to rob it as well but waited until you were back out on the road before arresting you. How far away is your home or final destination? We may need to provide you with an escort."

I told him I lived about a mile away, just on the other side of Rock Creek. He then responded, "Okay, that probably will be fine, but I'd like to ask you to park your truck there and don't drive it for the rest of the evening so we don't make this mistake again."

With great relief, I said, "Gladly." I got back into my truck and, as if it were an old friend I was talking to, said to it, "Well, this is another fine mess you've gotten me into." I guess you might say that my friend, the red Dodge pickup, had been the victim of profiling that evening based on the color of its paint!

That next day at work, I couldn't wait to tell the faculty and staff about my hair-raising experience that evening. When the word got out, Chris Szatkowski, our superintendent's administrative assistant, told her husband, whom I knew well and who happened to be a police officer in Lawton. He came to the school later that day to have lunch with his wife and gave me a hard time about it. He said, "So you were the poor guy they were talking about on all the dispatch radios. We all felt so sorry for you because they really thought they had their man! It's just a good thing you didn't give them any lip, because they were not in a mood for someone with an attitude." I learned later from him that one of the officers was an Oklahoma Highway patrolman and the other a deputy sheriff. I was too scared to even notice. All I remember is that they were in uniforms and had real guns!

The old Dodge eventually just got too expensive to keep running, and me not being an auto mechanic, I found it more and more difficult to find someone who would work on it. So reluctantly, I sold it to a good friend I knew would take great care of her. Greg Pierce, the superintendent of Pontotoc Technology Center in Ada, whom I had known for a long time, said that he and his son would like to completely restore it. That was something I knew I would never be able to do myself, so I sold it to him with a tear in my eye. That truck and I had literally grown up together, and now, after all these years, we were parting company. I still miss her today and often reminisce about the great times we had working and playing together. What a great truck she was.

Stories about my other fishin' trucks aren't nearly as intense as the experience we had in Cache that one evening, but nonetheless, all my trucks were unique vehicles that I bonded with throughout the course of my ownership with them, mostly as a result of the multiple fishing trips we had together. Fishin' truck number two was a blue 1980 Volkswagen diesel pickup. I was attracted to this truck because one, it had a diesel engine and would make about fifty miles to the gallon, which in those days had great appeal to me, and two, it was a front-wheel drive, which I thought was kind of neat. Basically, this was a pickup truck built on the same Rabbit chassis that VW had sold a ton of during the late 1970s and most of the '80s. It was quite functional as a fishing truck and still had enough power (just barely) to pull my bass boat to Lake Carl Blackwell, a nearby local lake west of Stillwater that I fished frequently. At the time, we had a trailer hitch on our family van, which was a full-size model and had a powerful V8 engine that was more than adequate to pull the boat on the longer fishing trips, so I had all my bases covered with regard to getting the bass boat to any lake I wanted. It was a good truck, although wintertime starting could be a challenge when the temperature dipped into the teens and I couldn't find a place to plug in the engine block heater. But it got me to all the farm ponds I wanted to go to at a fraction of the cost of the big Dodge.

The one experience that I had with it that stands out even though it's not directly related to fishing is the time I went to the pecan grove on my parent's farm to cut some firewood for the winter. I loaded the small bed to the top and headed home.

But the first time I came to a soft spot in the pasture, the tiny rear wheels started sinking into the ground from all the weight of the freshly-cut wood. It was then I first began to realize why most pickup trucks are rear-wheel drive. As the rear wheels began to sink, the front wheels, which powered the vehicle, raised just enough to where the vehicle was unable to get any traction as the drive wheel spun just above the surface of the ground. As I stood there stuck, I had two options. One was to swallow some pride and walk to Dad's house and ask him to get the farm tractor and pull me out, all the time knowing he was laughing inside his head and thinking to himself, *What kind of farm kid did I raise? Didn't have enough sense to buy a real pickup truck.* Now Dad would never say something like that to my face, because he was just too nice of a person to do such a thing, but I know he would have probably been thinking it. A second option was to unload half of the logs and hope the rear wheels would rise just enough for the front wheels to get sufficient traction to get out. I would then return for the rest of the firewood later. I opted for the latter and managed to pull out of the soft spot.

Following the sale of the Volkswagen pickup in 1994, I experimented with using as my primary fishing vehicle a class of trucks the auto industry calls sport utility vehicles (SUVs). A 1995 four-wheel drive forest green Jeep Grand Cherokee was my vehicle of choice during this period, and while it served its purpose well of pulling a boat and getting me anywhere I wanted to fish, I still missed having all the advantages of a pickup. Having a vehicle with four-wheel drive was something I especially liked in my Jeep, and I knew that from that point on, all my future fishing vehicles would be 4×4s. Eventually I tired of not having a pickup bed, and in 2000, I traded it off for one of the first four-door mass-produced pickups that went on the market, a silver four-wheel-drive Nissan Frontier. Wow, this had the best of both worlds. It could comfortably haul four passengers and still had a bed where the owner could put all his or her stuff. It got quite a few second looks as I drove it around because at the time, most pickups were two-door models. Nowadays, four-door pickups have become so popular that I do a double take when I see a late model with only two doors. Now I could haul all my gear plus three fishing buddies to the river or lake. And while I had dearly loved my pickups of the past, two strikes they had against them was their tendency to get stuck in muck and mud and their inability to carry more than one passenger. The Frontier was my first four-wheel drive pickup, and was I ever grateful at times to have it.

The first time this became apparent was on a trip my son Jim and I took to eastern Oklahoma when looking for place to catch running white bass during their spawn. We got some directions at a local bait shop that took us into a pasture behind a dam. All of a sudden, I could feel my rear wheels spinning, and sure enough, we were stuck. In the past when this happened to me with two-wheel drive pickups, there was little hope for anything other than to summon help from someone who had a tractor. But we were out in the middle of nowhere and didn't know who we would be able to turn to for help. Then I remembered, *Hey, I paid a little extra for this truck to get four-wheel drive. Let's see if it really makes a difference.* I grabbed the little shifter just to the left of the big one, pulled it down to the 4wd indicator light, and presto, we pulled that puppy right out of trouble and saved the fishing trip. Since that experience, I refuse to have anything but a four-wheel-drive system in my pickup.

The next fishin' truck I purchased was an orange 2005 Chevrolet Colorado. Being an OSU Cowboys fan, I absolutely loved the color and styling of this truck. It was a little larger than the Nissan Frontier, which I also liked. But this was my "bad luck" vehicle, and three experiences stick out that will always make me refer to it as the "bad luck truck." The first one was on a trip to Red River, New Mexico, that my wife Cindy and I took. Actually, we never got to our destination because of a kidney stone I got on the first evening of the trip. It resulted in an unplanned trip home, where I turned over the keys to Cindy and told her to drive like the wind back to Oklahoma, hoping we'd get stopped by a highway patrolman who could safely escort us to an emergency room in the nearest town, where I could get some relief. If you've ever had a kidney stone, then you know what I'm talking about. If you haven't, pray that you never will. They are that painful. They feel as if someone is sticking a knife in your side and then slowly turning the blade. Ouch! Anyway, I've never had the nerve to ask Cindy how fast that little truck would go, but she eventually got me to Boise City, Oklahoma, in a big-time hurry and to a doctor who gave me a shot of painkiller, and we were on our way back to OKC, where I later gave birth to a strapping young kidney stone in my bathroom!

The second bad luck story happened the very next year on a return trip to Red River on an excursion over some of the worst washboard roads you'll find anywhere on this planet as we pushed onward toward the Shuree Ponds on the Valle Vidal of the Carson National Forest. As the sun began to set, Cindy and I headed back to try to make it to the cabin before it got dark. About midway, I heard the dreaded pop of a blown tire. The road was narrow, and if another vehicle had come by, I'm not sure how it could have passed us. With this being a relatively new truck, I had no idea where the jack was, so I quickly got out the owner's manual and learned that the jack and jack handle were in two different, hard-to-get-to locations—a tribute to American designers who still have a thing or two to learn from the Japanese about making customer-friendly vehicles. The rear of the truck was loaded with gear and equipment, so we had to take everything out and put it in the bed of the truck just to get to the jack and jack handle. Of course, the spare was located under the bed of the truck, and it took a while to lower it down for removal.

All this time, it was getting dark, and I didn't have a working flashlight on me. Fortunately, the spare had sufficient air, and I got the tire changed about the same time it got dark. Now, I don't think she'll mind me saying this, because we all have our phobias, but Cindy is terribly afraid of bears and the entire time was looking around for an attacking bear that may have been looking for an easy meal. I tried to convince her that the only bears in these parts were black bears and that they fed primarily on berries and honey, but that didn't seem to matter much. She was sure that we were on their menu. At any rate, dealing with her wanting to get back safely on the road before the bears spotted us put even more pressure on me to get the tire changed as quickly as possible.

The third bad luck story came as I was taking grandson Nathan from our house in Oklahoma City to Stillwater to fish my parents' farm pond. Nathan had come up from Texas to visit us for a few days and get in a lot of fishing with Grandpa. We had it all planned. My mom was going to make her great-grandson's favorite meal (fried chicken on the bone, as he called it) and then we would go to the family farm pond for some bass fishing—only we never made it. We were somewhere between Oklahoma City and Guthrie, driving in a heavy rainstorm, when all of a sudden we hydroplaned and began spinning out of control. I'll never forget the look on Nathan's face as we spun what must have been several times before coming to rest on the center median.

Now, I am, If I don't say so myself, a very safe driver, and I had already reduced my speed to about 50 mph and even moved over into the left lane, where there was less water ponding. An even then, there were cars passing me on the right that must have been going 65 mph or better. After we eventually stopped spinning and came to a halt, I called Mom and told her about the situation and said that we were not going to be able to be there for lunch and fishing. I then called the highway patrol and a wrecker to address the situation we were in. Nobody was hurt, and we were so lucky that the truck hadn't spun into another vehicle or crossed the median into path of oncoming traffic.

The Oklahoma Highway Patrolmen working the case had some serious deficiencies in customer-relations skills and treated me as if I were a criminal speeding out of control during hazardous weather conditions. He gave me a ticket that I later got overturned in court. In doing my internet research, I learned that hydroplaning can occur at any time in these kinds of situations and that my speed at the time was totally within reason for the existing road conditions. And I had even put on new tires just a few weeks earlier as well. We were just unlucky, and evidently the judge concurred with my assessment. The main reason we didn't spin out of control and into oncoming traffic was because of a barrier that had been installed just for that purpose. Of course, my truck was totaled from hitting that barrier, and while I wasn't quite ready to trade off the Colorado, I didn't have a choice and soon purchased my next fishin' truck, a dark gray 2010 Honda Ridgeline.

Now, this truck had all the bells and whistles, and from a pragmatic point of view, it was the best pickup yet in terms of meeting my fishing needs. American designers could learn a thing or two from Japan in truck design. First, there was a spacious trunk located underneath the pickup bed that was bigger than those in many of the sedans I had previously owned. Second, the spare was located in this trunk, where it would always stay clean and easy to get to. And guess what? Unlike the Chevy Colorado, the jack and jack handle were together and right there next to the spare where they ought to be in the first place! My new Honda, being a crossover pickup, also rode more like a sedan than a truck, and in the ten years I owned it, I never heard any complaints from my rear-seat passengers during the long nine-hour trips to my cabin in Red River, New Mexico, about how uncomfortable the seats were. These complaints were pretty common in both the Frontier and the Colorado, which had seats that were nearly perpendicular, similar to the very rear seats of a jet airliner—the ones you can't recline. The Ridgeline was also a little bigger, and my Hobie Cat Kick Boat fit perfectly in the bed, which didn't have any space taken up by intruding rear wheel wells. The Hobie could never lie flat in the bed of either the Frontier or the Colorado because of those darned wheel wells. So it was the perfect vehicle for all my fishing needs.

I did have one unforgiveable experience with it, however, that will forever be etched in my brain. It left me sitting one time in the middle of nowhere in Slapout, Oklahoma, during a return trip from Red River with two of my fishing buddies. And yes, there is a Slapout; look it up. I elaborate on this unfortunate incident in chapter 11 of my first book, so I won't take time now to repeat the story; I will say only that I never quite felt the same about this truck from that point on, and I traded it two years later for the truck of my dreams—an orange-and-black 2020 Jeep Gladiator.

In many ways, a Jeep truck makes no sense for me to own other than that I first fell in love with Jeep pickups dating back to my days as a boy fishing with Cousin A. B. when we would take his dad's maroon 1948 Willys Jeep pickup to nearby farm ponds. There was something about the aura of that Jeep's classic shape and personality that told me early on,

"Someday I'm going to own one of these." That love affair was reinforced when I was in the Oklahoma Army National Guard and drove a military Jeep with an open top all the way from the armory in Stillwater, Oklahoma, to Ft. Carson, Colorado, where we were doing our two weeks of annual training. I had an opportunity that summer to be the driver for the training NCO. I loved every minute of that long, rough ride. Part of my driving responsibilities included driving to all the training sites on the military installation to make sure they were ready for classes and training exercises. One such trip included regular visits to Engineer Lake, where the water purification unit was. If only I could have taken a pack rod for that trip!

Unfortunately, in 1964 Jeep quit making its classic pickup that was styled along the same boxy lines of the original military jeep, and I thought all hope was lost for ever having a brand-new one someday. That hope resurfaced briefly with the introduction of the two-door Jeep Scrambler pickup in 1981, but it, too, was discontinued just five years later. During that same time, I was in the middle of raising a family, and a two-passenger pickup truck wasn't very practical for a four-person family.

But in 2019, the dream of someday owning a Jeep pickup became very real when the Jeep Gladiator, based on the popular Jeep Wrangler, hit the showroom floors. It didn't take me very long to purchase one and fulfill a lifelong dream. My new Jeep rides much rougher than the Ridgeline. It doesn't have an under-the-bed trunk and has a spare tire that will be difficult and dirty to dislodge from its under-the-bed location should I ever have a flat. The wind noise often keeps me from listening to the premium sound system when I'm bucking a headwind, and I suspect that I will begin to hear complaints from my fishing buddies again about how uncomfortable the rear perpendicular seats are. But you know what? That doesn't matter! I love my new Jeep all the same and just feel good driving it. I guess love doesn't always have to be practical—in this case, a love that began as a boy riding with Cousin A. B. in my uncle's 1948 Willys Jeep pickup. And guess who the first passenger not named Cindy was to ride in it with me? A. B. I had only driven it off the showroom floor a few days earlier when there was a Trout Unlimited meeting held one evening. I called A. B. on his cell phone and offered to pick him up at his house in Edmond and go to the meeting together. He accepted, and the twenty-minute ride from his house to the TU meeting in Oklahoma City was truly a trip down memory lane. I was driving this time instead of A. B. The Jeep was a 2020 model rather than a 1948. And it was orange and black rather than solid maroon. But the two principal characters were the same, just a few years older—fishing buddies who had treasured one another for over sixty years!

CHAPTER 11

GUIDES

The first time I ever used a guide was on the San Juan River when I was in my late forties. I was invited by John Hugon, a member of our state board of career-tech education, to go with him and two of his fishing buddies to the San Juan River in New Mexico. I drove to Duncan, Oklahoma, and met John and his two friends at the local airport to get on his company plane. From there we flew to Farmington, where we met a guide from Rizzuto's Fly Shop who drove us to the lodge. It was an absolutely splendid experience, and that's when I learned about dropper systems, how to use strike indicators (i.e., interest monitors), and how to mend my line to get the perfect drift. It was like going to school, only a whole lot more fun. It was also my first time in a drift boat. We switched guides each of the three days we were out on the water, and while each one was very knowledgeable; each guide had a unique way of teaching us techniques that worked on the San Juan. I learned so much during that trip and realized that if I was going to get serious about being a good fly-fisher, I needed to start hiring guides. Since then, I've fished with all kinds of guides from Argentina to Alaska, and

I have learned a great deal from all of them. For me they were like my college professors at Oklahoma State University on my way to obtaining a bachelor's degree, only this degree was in fly-fishing and was a whole lot more fun!

Guides are an interesting group, and I have yet to hire one that I didn't like and respect for his knowledge of the fish we were pursuing. Except for the bass fishing guide I did not hire, whom I discuss in great detail in chapter 7, they were all folks I would enjoy fishing with on a regular basis. And if you ask enough questions, each one of them has a plethora of information to share, along with enough interesting stories to make for an interesting and very entertaining book if he ever decided to write one.

I've always taken a great deal of pride in the journals I've kept since 1963. The fishing information has proven on many occasions to be the difference between having a productive or nonproductive day on the water. As I've gotten older, the reflection part of each journal entry has gotten a little more elaborate and detailed. But one item I regret not including in my logs on the earlier guided trips are names and contact information of the guides I fished with. I do a better job of that now, but for some reason I just didn't think it was important to include that important information in those early journal entries.

One day, in an effort to break the ice with a guide who didn't talk much, I asked what his most interesting experience was with a client. I had so much fun with that question that I began asking that same question on every guided trip I took. For example, one of the San Juan guides had a particularly interesting experience with a husband-and-wife team. He said he dreaded booking married couples because sometimes he felt more like a marriage counselor than he did a fishing guide, and too many times the entire trip was compromised by marital disharmony. He then began to tell me of one experience with a Mr. and Mrs. that went something like this. The guide asked the typical first question: "Have either of you ever fly-fished before?"

The husband responded, with a firm grip on his ego, "Yes, I have many times, so don't worry about me; just make sure my wife gets into some fish. I'll do just fine on my own."

The guide, with his face hidden to the client, just rolled his eyes and politely said, "You bet. I'll make sure she has every opportunity to have a productive day, but if you need anything or have any questions, just let me know."

"I won't, but thanks anyway," he replied in a confident tone.

Well, it wasn't long until the wife began catching one fish after another. After the fourth nice trout, the guide suggested to the husband that he might want to try the pattern they had been having success with and even volunteered, "If you don't have something similar in your vest, I'd be glad to give you one."

With even more resolve, but showing some signs of frustration, the spouse said, "Oh no. Really, I know what I'm doing. I was probably fly-fishing when you were still in diapers. I'm just doing a little experimenting right now with some different patterns. I'll be just fine. You just concentrate on my wife."

Another hour or so passed, and the perceptive wife, seeing her husband having no success at all and wanting him to get in on some of the fun, said something that served as the first shot over the bow. "Honey, why don't you let our guide help you catch some fish like he's helping me. You'll have so much more fun."

The husband responded with anger, "Are you implying that you know more about fishing than I do?"

"No," she said with emphasis. "It's just that he's an expert on this river and knows what he's doing."

"Like I don't?" the husband shouted back with some added rage to his tone of voice.

"Yes, that's exactly what I mean," she responded, and then, to add more fuel to the fire she added, "Lighten up and have some fun. You said I would enjoy fishing, and I have, but it's pretty obvious that you're not having much fun."

By this time, the guide was looking for a hole to crawl into because he knew the domestic war was escalading at a pace that wasn't going to have a happy ending, and he didn't know what to say or how to stop it. Finally, the husband, in absolute frustration, shouted at the guide, "That's it! Take me to shore. I'm getting off and walking back to the lodge."

The guide responded, "But sir, the lodge must be over three miles away from here, and it's over some pretty rough terrain."

The male client responded, "Who's paying your fee? Let me off now or I'll jump out and swim to shore. I've had all the lip I'm going to take from both of you, and I certainly don't need your advice to have a good time." The guide rowed the drift boat to shore, helped the client unload his gear and apologized as best he could for the unfortunate experience. He and the client's wife, at her insistence, continued to fish the rest of the day.

I asked him how the wife was from that point on, and he said she was just fine and related to him that her husband had an ego that could fill the Grand Canyon and that he would be fine after a few scotch and sodas and some time to cool down. She apologized for his behavior and said, "Just keep me into fish. There's no reason why I can't have a good time out here." The guide said that he had avoided husband-and-wife teams ever since if at all possible. I wanted to ask what kind of tip he got that day but thought some things are better left unanswered.

One of the nicest and most sensitive guides I ever had was Ed Adams out of Questa, New Mexico. I talk about Ed a little bit in my first book, *If It Were Easy, They'd Call It Catchin'*, but his awareness to client needs exceeded all expectations I had the day he guided me and two other anglers, Cousin A. B. and a good friend, Chuck Nithman, on the Cimmaron River in New Mexico. This was the trip where I had broken my leg the day before on a hike to a favorite fishing hole on the Rio Grande, which at the time I thought was just a bad sprain. Immediately after the fall, I conveniently found a staff, custom made by a resident beaver, that served as a pretty good crutch to help me get around. I conveniently called it "Wilson" after the soccer ball that assisted the character marooned on an island and played by Tom Hanks in the movie *Cast Away*. Ed took special care of me that day, placing me in all the best spots so I wouldn't have to move much to catch fish.

I recall that on one occasion, I lost Wilson as I struggled to move to another fishing spot while Ed was working with A. B. and Chuck. When he came by to check on me sometime later, he saw me limping along to get from one place to another. He asked me, "Where's Wilson?"

I thought to myself, *He must have heard me at some point refer to the beaver-made crutch from the Rio Grande as Wilson. How cool is that?* I said, "Oh, I must have left him there a ways back. I saw a good-looking hole I wanted to fish, and I accidently dropped it down the bank when I tried to get to the hole, and it was just too difficult for me to retrieve on one leg. I'll find another natural staff somewhere and keep going."

Ed responded, "Oh you can't leave Wilson behind; he's your good luck charm. How far back do you think you lost it?" I estimated how far back it was, and Ed promptly hiked down river to look for it. It wasn't long before he came back, all smiles, and said, "Look who I found lying there by a steep bank? Wilson!" I've got to tell you, that effort on Ed's part meant more to me than he'll ever know. That very same makeshift crutch is hanging in my man cave today with the name "Wilson" proudly framed under it as a memorial to that trip and one of the nicest and most sensitive guides I've ever had the pleasure to fish with.

Another guide who went above and beyond in making sure I had a great experience was Matt Bickford out of Bath, Maine. Matt was my guide on the Kennebec River and got me into some really nice striped bass fishing, with the biggest one going twenty-seven inches. He was employed by L.L. Bean in nearby Freeport and had only one day to guide that week, which was disappointing because I had hoped to try my luck for some smallmouth bass the following day.

After a great day of fly-fishing for stripers, I casually asked him if he knew of a good smallmouth bass fishery that I could fish on my own the next day. He didn't hesitate and told me about two easy-to-access places on the Androscoggin River that were both less than thirty miles away from my hotel in Bath. He even offered to text me both locations to make sure I found them.

Later that evening, I got a text from him with both locations pinned, complete with the best fishing spots highlighted on each Google Earth photograph. I drove to the first location, took a short hike to the river, and got into some great smallmouth bass fishing, as though I had the benefit of Matt's expertise for two full days but only paid for the price of one. What a great experience with someone who really wanted to make sure I had a fantastic trip to brag about to my fishing buddies back home.

I've always felt that the sign of a really good guide is one who is resourceful enough to get you into fish despite the conditions. One such guide was Simon Becker. Simon was probably the most famous guide I'd ever fished with. He is featured in Orvis publications and is the creator of the highly successful HoverCrab. I went to Key West, Florida, in December to try to land some bonefish or permit, which were both on my bucket list. The weather was absolutely gorgeous, with highs in the mid-eighties every day. According to Simon, ideal conditions for permit and bonefish fishing is sunny weather with a light wind—the sun to be able to see the fish better and the wind so they don't see us as well. But the only day I had to fish, we had neither. I did throw to one tailing permit he saw, but it being my first cast and all, for such a wary species, I cast a little too far, and the line hit him across his back and he spooked. This type of sight fishing, in my opinion, is about as challenging as fishing gets.

After a few hours of not even throwing to a single fish, Simon, sensing my frustration, asked me if I wanted to get into some action regardless of species, and I said, "Yes, that would be great." After all, isn't it all really about just getting your pole bent? Simon knew his business well enough to know exactly where to go for some great crevalle jack action, and that afternoon, I caught five of these powerful fish. We used a #2 Simon Becker HoverCrab, which he made famous, and it ended up being a very fun trip that resulted in a lot of great pictures of me holding some nice crevalle jacks. These are fun fish and fight deep and hard, similar to the freshwater channel cat I catch back in Oklahoma. Simon, unlike some other guides that I had encountered, was able to make lemonade out of lemons, and he wound up with a very happy client. Some guides don't seem to know how to do that.

And while it doesn't happen often, you sure remember those times when you paid a guide good money and went back home without any fish to show for it. It's only happened twice to me: once when fly-fishing for stripers on Lake Texhoma, and again for redfish along the Texas gulf coast. Both times I left those trips with not the best feeling about my guide's expertise regardless of how much fun I had by just being out on the water. On those two outings, the fish pitched a perfect game: no hits, no runs, no errors, and no one left on base. But just like the carnie barking from his booth on the midway at the state fair likes to say, "You pays your money and you takes your chances."

Probably the biggest compliment I ever received from a guide was from a US Marine-veteran-turned-fishing-guide, on the Bighorn River in Montana. I regret not recording his full name in my journal, but I do recall that his first name was Rob. Rob was one of the nicest guides I'd ever fished with and was a great conversationalist. Spending a day on the water with Rob was like fishing with my best friend. During a brief lull in the fishing, I asked him if he minded if I tried one of my Ginger Buggers that I had designed and tied myself. He said, "Sure, you're the client." To my delight, I immediately began to see some action. I showed it to him and asked him if he wanted one and he enthusiastically said yes. We had been having good action on brown trout all day using his flies, so I wasn't sure how'd he react to me offering him one of mine, but he seemed thrilled, and seeing him react that way certainly made my day and was nearly as rewarding as catching all the fish he had gotten me into on that trip.

And speaking of nice guides, one that I will always remember is a guide from Argentina. Here again, I didn't write down his full name in my journal, but I did indicate in my entry for that trip that his first name was Pepe. Pepe did an excellent job of getting us into some big rainbows in four different rivers in Patagonia, but the experience I remember the most is when he wanted me and my fishing mate Scott Spradling to meet his family. After we had finished fishing, Pepe drove us to the local feed-and-seed store in San Martin that his family owned. His wife was very attractive and had gorgeous blue eyes to go along with her equally beautiful olive-toned skin. We had a great conversation with both of them, as their English was very good. On the way back to our hotel, Pepe asked us if we noticed that the color of his wife's eyes was blue. We both told him that we had indeed noticed that unique feature. He winked at us and said, "I think there's a little Nazi blood on her side of the family." It was also her cooking that we enjoyed each day as part of our shore lunch, and, as someone of German descent myself, I could certainly taste some of that ethic heritage in those wonderfully prepared meals she made for us.

Another interesting guide that I fondly remember is one that we had on the Middle Fork of the Salmon River. This was a five-day wilderness float trip, and our guides were more whitewater guides than fishing guides, but we still caught fish in pristine water that is rarely encountered by humankind. Each evening, as we gathered around the campfire with our adult beverages, one of the guides would be in charge of entertaining us with either a story or something of interest about the local surroundings we were encountering on the float trip. One of them told us about the life of privilege he had grown up in as part of a wealthy family in Boston. He recalled his family's great displeasure when he announced to them that he was going to be a history major in college. They asked, "What are you going to do with a degree in history? Teach?"

"Exactly," he said.

He went on to say that he had come from a large family who were typically lawyers, doctors, engineers, or successful entrepreneurs who were all highly successful with handsome incomes. Four years later, when he told his parents that he had accepted a job to teach history at a local public high school, they practically disowned him. After a few years of teaching history and having to put up with all the humiliation every Thanksgiving, Christmas, and Easter, when the inevitable comparisons were being made by his parents, uncles, and aunts to his siblings and cousins about their successful careers, along with their recent purchases of luxury automobiles, vacation properties, and stock portfolios, he told his parents he'd had enough. He had made the decision to resign from his teaching position and go to Idaho and live off the grid for a year. His parents threatened to deprive him of his inheritance if he did such a thing, which only served to increase his resolve to leave. He found an abandoned log cabin in the Rockies and lived there for a year just to prove to himself he could do it. Somewhere along the way, he learned how to fly-fish, tie flies, and carve knife handles from deer and elk antlers. To get by, he sold his knives and hand-tied flies to local outfitters and did some guiding on the local rivers. He's never been back to Boston since, although he occasionally makes the obligatory holiday phone call to his parents, who still don't understand him and his ways, but he told us he has no plans to ever go back east to the world he grew up in—one he never really liked very much.

The guides I had on a trip to Alaska had a story that was similar but not nearly so dramatic. Two brothers were farmers in Iowa, where they grew corn. Each year they struggled to make ends meet as farmers, but they would always put away enough money to treat themselves to a family vacation to Alaska because they loved to fly-fish and their families all loved going there. One summer, they noticed that the fly-in lodge they always stayed in was up for sale. After talking to their wives in what had to have been an extremely interesting conversation, they all decided to sell both their farms and throw caution to the wind and buy the lodge. They moved to Anchorage, where they live during the off-season, and they move out to the lodge during the summer months, where they manage the facility and provide guide service on the Talachuletna River. The year I was there, one of their sons was my guide. He was a wonderful young man who reminded me so much of my own son, Jim. I asked him if he ever thought his dad ever longed for the days of being an Iowa farmer, and he quickly responded, "I don't think for one second." Both the Iowa farmers and the young man from Boston, could serve as poster children for "living the dream!" It kind of makes you wonder what's wrong with the rest of us.

And since this chapter is about fishing guides, I feel compelled to say a few words about my very dear friend Bruce Gray, who used to guide on Oklahoma's Eufaula Lake just outside Stigler. Bruce taught marketing education at Stigler High School, and to help with the family finances, he would guide during the weekends and summer months. He told me that he made nearly as much money guiding as he did teaching. While I obviously never had the occasion to hire Bruce as a guide, I never realized what a fringe benefit it was to have a best friend who was also a fishing guide. Bruce and I fished together many times, and each time I was out with him, I realized why he was so good at guiding. First, he knew so much about bass fishing that it seemed as though he had done a doctoral dissertation on the subject. And second, he had the type of engaging personality that made me want to be with him all day. He could relate to anybody regardless of his or her station in life, from the corporate boardroom to the shop floor. That's why he was so successful in his professional career. The national headquarters for the Distributive Education Clubs of America (DECA) hired Bruce away from Oklahoma to develop and organize a fundraising effort for the construction of a new national headquarters to be built in Reston, Virginia. In only three years, Bruce wined and dined folks in both the public and private sectors and raised enough funds to build the National DECA Center. After the project was completed, he came back to Oklahoma to be the superintendent and CEO for the Great Plains Technology Center in Lawton, Oklahoma, where he hired me to join his administrative team in 1978. He was later recruited to assume that same position at the state's premier career-tech center, Francis Tuttle Technology Center in Oklahoma City, the same exact place and position I would eventually wind up in until my retirement in 2019. My career in public school administration blossomed from that first administrative job at Great Plains, and I was forever indebted to him for that opportunity at age thirty. I know I was too young for that type of responsibility, but Bruce took a chance on me, and it changed my life forever.

I have to share this one story that will give you a little insight into Bruce's personality. Bruce loved to rag on his friends, and we never seemed to mind because he was so good at it and he would do it only to those he loved dearly. On a trip to Canada, I thought I would impress everyone with a purchase of a spinning reel that I knew nobody would ever have and had probably never seen before. This was back in the days before I converted to fly-fishing, so fellow fly-fishing fanatics, stay with me for a while as I tell this story. The reel was a Mepps Super Meca, which was built like a Sherman tank, imported from France, and had a lifetime guarantee. It looked like no other spinning reel I had ever seen before and had a skirted spool design, which at the time was revolutionary. It was the smoothest-running reel I had ever used but was really too big and too heavy to be very practical, and with its odd styling, it would never become mainstream like the

French-made Mitchells or the German-made Quicks, which were the popular choices of many spin fishermen back then. The first day I was in the boat with Bruce, I couldn't wait to show it off and get his reaction. Surely this professional guide and national Strike King field tester would raise an eyebrow and give me some street cred. But here's how the conversation went. I started out by saying, "Hey Bruce, look at my new reel." With a somewhat bewildered look on his face he responded, "Tommy Bill! What in the world is that?" I proudly went in to all its features and even told him how much I had paid for it. He then said, "Let me try it out."

With even more pride, I handed it over to him for a few test casts. Surely he would be as impressed with it as I was and utter a few "Wows" and "Oh My Goshes," sprinkled with a "This reel is incredible," followed by a "Where can I get one?" At last I finally had something that Bruce would envy the entire time we were in Canada. Instead, this is what I got after a few casts: After visually studying its odd design, he said, "You paid how much for this?"

I sheepishly confessed "$49.50," which at that time was a small fortune for a spinning reel.

"Forty-nine dollars and fifty cents?" he asked again, just to make sure.

"Yep," I said, but now with a little bit of reservation.

"Well, I wish I could have been there to see that, because that was a deal where two fools met. One who thought they could sell it, and another one who actually bought it." Then he started that infectious laugh that only Bruce could do, and I found myself laughing just as hard. It was his way of saying, "I love you, buddy."

My last story isn't about a guide but rather about a pilot of a bush plane, but since he was part of the hired staff for a fishing trip and because I don't have enough stories to fill a chapter about bush pilots, I'm going to include it here. It was on one of our fishing trips to Ontario, and we all decided that we wanted to catch tiger muskies, which are a hybrid of the muskellunge and northern pike. It is a rare occurrence in the wild, but we were told about a lake that held a bunch of them, though it could be accessed only by float plane. The fishery was Kishkutena Lake. We hired a float plane to take us there and met it at a boat dock for loading. We put so much stuff in his de Havilland Beaver that I thought to myself, *We'll never get airborne. I hope this pilot knows what he's doing. Surely he would tell us if we have the plane overloaded. But then how would he know? Nothing has been weighed like they do at all the airports. Surely the margin of error is much smaller for bush planes than for those big commercial jets.* So it was just a leap of faith as we kept putting more and more gear into the Beaver.

The outfitter we had contracted with told us they would have four aluminum V-hull boats on this one island, and all we had to do was provide four small outboard engines, our tents, and food for our four-day stay on the island, so you can imagine how much gear the eight of us had, plus those tents and outboards. As luck would have it, I got to sit up front with the pilot and would have the perfect seat to observe every detail of some of the most gorgeous scenery on earth. I was excited. We made a few preliminary runs on the water, and just as we were getting revved up to make our run to get airborne, I noticed that none of the instruments in front of me were working. Well, I'm no pilot, but I have driven a car, a boat, and a farm tractor many times and know that the manufacturer puts all those gauges in there for a purpose. And since I was sitting in the copilot's seat, I felt obliged to tell the pilot of the airplane about my keen observation that none of the damn gauges were working!

In a somewhat panicked tone, I asked, "Hey aren't these gauges supposed to be working?"

He calmly responded, "Oh, those! Darned things hardly ever work." He then made a fist with his right hand and began banging on the instrument panel, and presto, they all came on! He laughed, "Well, that rarely happens when I pound on them. Usually they just stay dead. You must be good luck! Heck, we're only flying a little bit above the treetops anyway. Don't really need any of them to work, including the fuel gauge, because I fill up before every trip."

I guess I was supposed to have taken some comfort from my little chat with the pilot, but I didn't enjoy the trip nearly as much as I could have if the doggone gauges would have worked in the first place and if I hadn't seen all the cargo we crammed into that plane. But what a great sense of humor displayed by the pilot. We arrived at our island safely and caught a ton of smallmouths, walleyes, and pike, but no tigers. It was a great trip, and I learned a lesson about bush pilots that day.

CARPIN'

think carp, a Chinese import, may be the smartest of all gamefish. At least for me, they are the hardest to figure out. I love to wade for these guys in the shallow flats of some of our Oklahoma lakes with my fly rod on my shoulder, looking for isolated puffs of suspended dirt in the water (a.k.a. mud puffs) or maybe an exposed tail in about two feet of water. It's a totally different type of fishing where you make a cast only when you see a fish or visual evidence that they are actually feeding. I love fishing Taylor Lake near Rush Springs, where there are long stretches of shoreline bordered by cattails. I'm constantly looking for feeding carp, but I'm also listening for them. There comes to mind no other type of fishing where I use so many senses. Carp are the only fish I know of that anglers can locate by using their sense of hearing. You can actually hear them sucking algae and moss off the cattails near the root line. When that happens, you know that's where they are and where you need to be. When I hear them, I then wade to that part of the shoreline and look for cattails moving from side to side as the result of their rigorous attempt to dislodge vegetation from the plant stems. Just like us, carp enjoy a little salad before their main course of animal protein (i.e., aquatic insects and worms). So I just wait a while for them to make their exit from the cattails and into open water. That's when I have my best chance to make a good presentation.

Casting into cattails without hanging up is a skill that I'm not sure any fly-fisher has ever developed. As soon as the carp exit the cattails and move into open water, there is a much better chance of getting a take, but still not a very good one. At this point, you can spook them either by the vibrations your feet make when wading to them, or from them seeing your shadow. Either will alert them that there is danger in the water, and they'll suddenly explode out toward the middle of the lake. I still jump every time they do that, because it always comes when I'm least expecting it, and the noise is similar to someone throwing a small boulder into the water. Ah, the sights and sounds of carp fishing!

They can also be easily spooked by a misguided cast that winds up with your fly line landing across their exposed back as you attempt to present the fly in their projected feeding path. And all this is in addition to the challenge we all have with any species we're targeting, and that's offering them something that they will accept as food. In my opinion, they can be as picky as any member of the salmonid family when it comes to fly selection. There have been times when I've thrown a half dozen patterns to the same tailing carp before I finally selected a fly that she perceived as something she wanted for lunch on that particular day.

Carp have their own unique beauty. And while the head, whiskers, and bugle-shaped mouth are features only a mother could love, the variety of bright orange to golden hues they display on their body and fins more than make up for it and can be downright breathtaking. Just hold one up to the sun sometime and let it shine through the fish's translucent fins and tell me you're not impressed by how pretty they are. The colors remind me of a harvest sunset in Oklahoma. I always enjoy seeing the expression of dyed-in-the-wool bass fishermen or snooty trout anglers when I tell them I fish for carp with a fly rod. Sometimes I don't think they believe me, but then I pull out my smartphone and start to show them pictures of some I've caught, often with a small fly still attached to their mouth. A common comment I hear is, "What! Carp will hit flies? What do you do with it after you've caught one?"

I respond, "The exact same thing I do with a rainbow trout: gently release it and wish it well."

Pound for pound, I'm not sure there is a more powerful fighter in all of the freshwater world. Not to be critical of largemouth bass, a species I dearly love and have been fishing for my entire life, but if you were to tie one end of a rope to the tail of a five-pound bass and the other to a five-pound carp, it wouldn't even be close. That carp would pull the poor bass from one end of the lake to the other! And a carp's stamina is beyond belief. Just about the time you think you've worn a big one down and get it close to the net, it just stares at you with those big eyes and says, "Not yet, buddy ... think I'll make another long run on ya. Hope the drag on your reel is up to it." I usually find myself making half a dozen landing attempts followed by long, powerful runs before I can finally net anything eighteen inches or bigger.

Carp also seem to have their own unique personalities. They are the only fish I know that will jump out of the water in the middle of the lake on a blistering hot summer afternoon for no apparent reason other than maybe they just think it's a lot of fun. It must take a lot of energy for a cold-blooded animal to get airborne in warm water, but they seem to enjoy it much in the same manner that dolphins do. Since we know they have the ability to jump, I can't figure out why they don't do it during the hook-up like trout, pike, and bass do. That would certainly add to the fighting dynamics of landing one of these brutes. Jumping might also increase their credibility with more anglers as a game fish, but for some reason, once hooked, they prefer to head out to the middle in deep water, much like a catfish would. But what a spectacular experience it would be if they would choose to combine their ability to jump with their sheer power. It'd be like catching a freshwater tarpon. But they are carp, for crying out loud, the self-actualized of the game fish world! They simply don't feel the need to impress anybody for any reason with their athleticism.

I received my first exposure to fly-fishing for carp from John Sievert from Edmond, Oklahoma—an angler I met on a fly-fishing message board, www.flyanglersonline.com. Another online fly-fisher, Robert McMahan from Altus, Oklahoma, was also a frequent poster on that board, and the three of us decided to physically meet each other on Taylor Lake near Rush Springs, Oklahoma, for some summertime bass fishing. We met at dawn and fished until it started getting really hot around noon. The bass weren't cooperating that day, but John noticed some feeding carp in the shallow flats and immediately switched to a pattern he had designed especially for carp and began catching some huge fish. The fly he was using was very simple, consisting of a chain head, olive chenille body, and an olive marabou tail tied on a size 10 hook. I didn't have one, of course, and didn't feel I knew John well enough to ask to borrow one of his.

I wished I would have packed some trout nymphs for the trip, but since we were targeting bass that day, I had left them at home. I searched the flies I had in my warm-water gear and noticed that I had a box of assorted bluegill flies that happened to contain a #8 bead-head Prince Nymph. So I tied one on, thinking at least it was a nymph pattern and maybe it would work. After making more casts than I care to remember to feeding carp who were aggressively making mud puffs, I finally convinced a cruiser (which normally aren't feeding fish) to do a ninety-degree turn and inhale the Prince. Go figure! Then the fight was on. It was my first carp, and it measured only twenty inches, but I was absolutely amazed by its power. I've been hooked on carp ever since. Thanks, John, for adding this species to my fishing agenda—one of the gamest fish you'll ever want to pursue on a fly rod.

I later went home and tied a duplicate of the fly John was using, and it's now my go-to carp fly. I've tried all the patterns that the experts say work best, but for me it's the pattern John designed that I keep going back to for consistent results.

One of my fishing heroes is Dave Whitlock, who loves pursuing carp with a fly rod. In the book *Carp on the Fly*, authored by Barry Reynolds, Brad Befus, and John Berryman, Dave specifically lists his favorite flies for carp, so he obviously treats them as a serious game fish. He goes on to say, "I choose my carp flies as carefully as if I were fishing for selective brown trout or spooky permit." I had the honor to personally meet Dave at a Trout Unlimited meeting in Midwest City, Oklahoma, several years ago, and when he heard I was a carpin' man, his eyes lit up like a little kid receiving his first fishing rod at Christmas. I guess we're still a pretty rare breed of fly-fishers. Of course, Dave is also a talented artist, and I purchased a print that evening from him depicting a smallmouth bass following a feeding carp in hopes of stealing a crayfish. He signed it with the following inscription: "Yours Tom, In Carpin & Smallmouthin. 9/15/15." That framed print is one of the most treasured items I have in the man cave.

As my infatuation with fly rod carpin' grew, I decided to make an exhaustive search for water that contained carp that was closer than the one-and-a-half-hour drive to Taylor Lake.

One frequently hears that carp are everywhere, and while they probably are, finding the right carp water for a fly-fisher can be a bit of a challenge. First, if you want to go wading for them in the flats, many of the lakes and ponds in central Oklahoma have soft bottoms that are not suitable for wading. In many cases, you will sink up to your knees in mud and muck that can grab you like quicksand, and your fishing trip turns into one of those *The Lone Ranger* episodes where the Lone Ranger is rescued from certain disaster by his trusty steed Silver, who pulls him to safety with a rope. But I don't normally ride a horse to my fishing destinations, so I have to be a little more selective in where I choose to fish. At any rate, an unstable lake bottom along the shoreline can create very undesirable fishing conditions and make it nearly impossible to wade and sight-fish. Remember: we're not talking about loading up a treble hook with dough bait and casting it with a Bubba rod and waiting for something to happen. This is fly-fishing in its purest form—persuading an intelligent fish that spooks at the slightest notion of anything that doesn't feel natural as well as being very picky as to the type of fly it might prefer on that particular day. I finally found the perfect water conditions in a chain of three ponds directly west of Lake Hefner below the dam, about ten minutes' driving time from my house when I lived in northwest Oklahoma City. At the time, these ponds were crystal clear and lined with cattails, which provided great cover when making presentations to tailing carp in the shallows. Even then, they were much spookier than the carp I had encountered at Taylor Lake, and most days I scared more off than I was able to cast to. It is here that I learned to be stealthy in my approach, and many times I would sneak up to them on my hands and knees, never standing up to make my cast. The Hefner ponds are in easy viewing distance of cars going up and down the Lake Hefner Parkway, and I can only imagine what must have been going through the minds of folks in their vehicles when they looked out their window and saw this weird person crawling near the shoreline with a fishing rod in his hand!

A twenty-seven-inch golden bonefish dwarfs my fly rod following a long battle in plain sight of motorists passing by on the Lake Hefner Parkway in OKC.

It is also on these ponds that I learned what dapping is. Dapping is a technique where you hold the rod directly over the fish and ever so gently just drop the fly into the water. You never have to worry about the fly line hitting the fish's back and spooking it, because the line never leaves the reel. Of course, this requires a long rod and, again, stealthily sneaking your way in close enough to drop the fly in front of her. For this technique, I prefer a ten-foot four- or five-weight fly rod. After doing this a few times, I realized that in crawling to get close enough to drop the fly in the carp's feeding zone, I was wearing holes in my pants and developing cuts and bruises on my knees from the sharp grass stick-ups and small rocks that I encountered. I went to Cabela's to see what they might have in the store as a remedy to this situation and found nothing. Undeterred, I then went to my local hardware store and purchased some knee pads that carpet installers often wear when they're putting new carpet in a home. Oh, the lengths we go to in the pursuit of the elusive and alluring fish we seek! The knee pads were relatively inexpensive and worked like a charm. Fishing for Hefner carp reminded me of an outdoor show I saw one time where bow hunters would use similar tactics to get close enough to pronghorn antelope in the flat plains of the Oklahoma panhandle where there is virtually no cover to hide the hunter from his or her prey.

Where I live now, in Edmond, Oklahoma, our backyard is bordered by a small lake that was created when a dam was built on Tinker Creek, a tributary to Lake Arcadia. I've noticed a lot of carp in the shallows sunbathing with their backs nearly exposed out of the water, and just like with their jumping antics, I have to ask myself, "Why do they do that?" Maybe they do it for the same reason we humans take in the sun—to get a nice tan (in their case giving them some nice golden fins). I've yet to see a carp hit a fly when it's sunbathing, or at least I haven't been successful in getting a take when they're doing that. And when I go in for a closer look, they shoot out like guided missiles, which startles the heck out of me.

But occasionally I will notice one feeding and stirring up mud with its tail exposed. That's when I get excited and run to the man cave to fetch a rod from the rack already rigged with my favorite carp fly—the one I learned about from carpin' buddy John Sievert. But the fish on my new pond are even spookier than the ones I used to belly crawl to at the Lake Hefner ponds.

One hot summer day in June, I noticed the carp were everywhere and actively feeding, and I decided to get serious about seeing if I could interest one in my fly. Since there were so many feeders this day, I totally sold out to Mr. Buglemouth. On the first six fish I threw to, I don't think I made more than three serious presentations. I either got hung up on submerged vegetation and spooked them trying to get the fly free, or I got a clump of moss on the fly before it made its way to where the carp was feeding. On other occasions, I would either make an errant cast that resulted in the line landing squarely on the fish's back and spooking it, or I would misjudge where the fish's head was and make a cast where the guide path of the fly never got close enough to its strike zone. Each time I made a bad cast or inappropriate presentation, the carp would let me know it with a sudden burst of speed to the middle of the lake that must have approached zero to sixty miles per hour in four seconds flat. Every time that happened, it would scare five years of life out of me, which meant I should have been dead from old age by about half past three that afternoon.

Finally, I made the money cast from a kneeling position, and the targeted carp shot straight out to the deep like there was no tomorrow with my fly firmly penetrated in her soft lips. It's a funny thing about carp—you never feel a strike, just sudden resistance, and this guy was no different. I can't tell you how excited I was to finally get one of these fish I had been seeing along my shoreline for so long to finally hit. After a twenty-minute fight with at least six false landing attempts during which I would get her close to the net only to see her come up with another burst of energy and make a long run to the deep, I managed to net her. I held the twenty-two-inch beauty up skyward and looked up at the sun through her bright golden fins and marveled at her spectacular glamour and unique beauty. This fish had more gold on her than most. No wonder they are often referred to by their fans as golden bonefish.

Finally tricked this twenty-two-inch beauty into taking my olive #10 John Sievert Carp Fly. Caught her just a short walk from the patio of my man cave.

CHAPTER 13

CATFISH ON THE FLY

The catfish family is another species of fish that doesn't get the respect it deserves in the fly-fishing community. My first big fish was a channel cat that I caught in my Uncle Chuck Voise's farm pond when I was just nine years old, using a minnow for bait. I remember it just as if it were yesterday. I can still hear the instructions I received that day from my dad—to just watch the red-and-white plastic bobber and, if it went under, to jerk the rod up and pull the fish in. I'm not sure he ever thought I'd actually catch a fish, but I'm sure he felt obliged to at least give me some basic instructions and let me give it a whirl. At best, I might be able to catch some small crappie or green sunfish that I could easily pull straight out of the water like Dad instructed. Dad hooked up the minnow, set the bobber, and then assisted me in casting the line out far enough to at least convince me I was officially fishing. He then left me to myself to visit with his brothers and sisters, who were all sitting in lawn chairs under a shade tree somewhere near the pond.

As I recall, it wasn't all that long before the bobber went under, and I did just as I had been instructed and pulled up on the rod to set the hook and lift the fish out of the water.

I followed those instructions perfectly, except nothing happened! It was as if I had hooked onto one of Uncle Chuck's Poland China hogs from the farm. I panicked and did what any boy would do my age, and that was to put the rod on my shoulder, turn my back to the water, and walk as fast as I could in the opposite direction, pulling whatever was on the other end out of the water and onto the shore. The fish was big (four pounds), but not big enough to challenge a tug-of-war with a highly motivated sixty-five-pound little boy (and his fifty-pound-test braided line) who was bound and determined to find out what in the world he had hooked.

This was during one of our big family get-togethers on Uncle Chuck and Aunt Elfrieda's farm near Perry, Oklahoma. The entire extended Friedemann/Voise clan had gathered there to celebrate Memorial Day. All the boy cousins and some of the uncles and aunts went down to Uncle Chuck's farm pond to do some fishing. My fish was the only channel cat caught and was by far the biggest fish of the day, so you can imagine how excited I was to outfish all my family (kids and adults.) That was the day I knew I wanted to be a fisherman, and that feeling of pride and youthful excitement comes back every time I catch a quality fish, even into my seventies. It's like I'm nine years old all over again. That was actually the first fish I ever logged, because I wanted to remember it for the rest of my life. I took the head after we cleaned it, coated it with a layer of salt, and nailed it to a wooden plaque my dad made for me out of some scrap lumber he had lying around. I really wanted to display it in my room, but that's where mom drew the line and said I had to keep it outside. So I proudly hung it on a wall in our barn. I looked at that channel cat head nearly every day for several years with a sense of pride and accomplishment that most nine-year-olds probably never get to feel today. I've had a soft spot for catfish ever sense.

My first-prize catch at age nine:
a four pound channel catfish.

I was very fortunate to have an older cousin, A.B., who lived on the farm just a mile from us and who was already into fishing and knew far more about the sport than I did at the time. So I had a built-in teacher whom I could rely on to instruct me in everything I needed to know about the sport. I learned how to fly-cast and how to use a spinning rig, and I eventually mastered the free-spool baitcasting reel. Soon I began logging all my catches. But I pretty much gave up fly-fishing by the time I was twelve and concentrated on using artificial lures for bass with conventional gear. I can't ever remember catching a catfish on an artificial lure during the time I was fishing primarily for largemouth bass. I had heard of channel cats being caught on artificial baits accidently when fishing for bass, but it never happened to me in the four decades I fished exclusively with spinning and baitcasting rigs. Then came the complete changeover to fly-fishing in 1994, and presto, I started catching catfish in significant numbers on flies. At first they were a pleasant surprise, but eventually I came to expect them when I was using bass flies and even when I focused on panfish with smaller patterns. Some of my largest channel cats have been caught on bluegill and crappie patterns no bigger than a size 12.

Much like carp, catfish are powerful fighters who never jump and prefer to stay deep. I don't believe they have the stamina of carp, but they can certainly match them in sheer power and, like carp, are much stronger than bass. Unlike carp fishing, I don't have special patterns that I prefer for them, although Woolly Buggers, Clouser Deep Minnows, spin flies, and crappie jigs seem to work best. Heck, I even caught a twenty-four-incher on a big #3/0 bass popper one time. My largest catfish ever was a twenty-eight-inch channel cat caught on a #2 orange-and-lime Woolly Bugger. I had just completed refurbishing an old South Bend bamboo fly rod that I bought on eBay and matched it to a vintage Bronson Royalist reel. The rig looked quite striking and took me back in time to the fifties. But I had always intended using it for light duty only—specifically bluegills.

One hot summer evening, I was invited by John Sievert to fish with him in his neighborhood pond in Edmond, Oklahoma, which he said held some huge bluegills. I thought this would be the perfect spot to have some bamboo fun. I tied on an orange-and-lime Woolly Bugger that I had made especially for sunfish. On one of the furthest casts I made all night, straight toward the middle, a huge channel cat nailed my fly the second it hit the water, just as if it had been hovering in that exact spot knowing that was precisely where the fly was going to land. I couldn't believe the size of the fish I had just hooked up with on my fragile bamboo rod rigged with a four-pound-test tippet. After a long, exhaustive fight that lasted about twenty minutes, I finally landed her without a net (who needs a net when you're bluegill fishing?) It was almost completely dark by that time, and I didn't have a flashlight of any kind, which made the landing even more difficult in a pond I wasn't familiar with. And by the way, have you ever tried to land a twenty-eight-inch channel cat in the dark bare-handed? I would never recommend it. To this day, I'm not sure how I avoided getting stuck with one of those three needle-sharp barbs they have!

A twenty-eight-inch channel catfish caught on a #2 Orange-and-Lime Woolly Bugger with a bamboo rod.

I think the smallest pattern I've used to catch one of my largest channel cats was a #12 Prince Nymph. Once again, I was bluegill fishing using a popper/dropper system when the twenty-four-inch cat went after the much smaller dropper. Mr. Whiskers will always surprise you when you least expect it.

Channel cats are not the only kind of catfish I've begun catching on a fly rod. One hot and humid summer evening, I was in my Hobie Cat kick boat, fishing along some riprap on Lake Hefner in northwest Oklahoma City, when I had a hard strike on a #3/0 orange-and-white Pistol Pete. Because she immediately went deep and fought hard, I assumed I had a nice channel cat on. As I began to finally wear her down, I noticed that she had a strange color to her. It wasn't until she made her first pass by the kick boat that I realized it wasn't a channel cat at all, but instead a flathead catfish! Talk about a shock! I mean, most of the flatheads I've ever read about were caught either noodling (a.k.a. hand fishing) or on jug lines with bait. I had no idea they would ever take a fly. What a treasure this particular fish was, given the reputation of her species for not hitting artificial baits. She measured eighteen inches in length.

I've also caught bullheads, the smaller cousins of the catfish family, which, like flatheads, have never been known for taking artificial baits. In Oklahoma, they're commonly referred to as mudcats, because of the reputation they have for being bottom feeders, but I offer proof that they will actively pursue and hunt down a properly presented fly as well. My parents used to love to eat these guys if I could catch them big enough to clean and prepare for the frying pan, and they swore that they were the best-tasting member of the catfish family. Having caught a ton of them as a boy on live worms for the family table, I can personally attest to their tastiness. The patterns I've been successful with for bullheads have usually had a spinner of some type in front of the fly, such as a Pistol Pete or a marabout streamer attached to an in-line spinner. All catfish have very limited vision, and I would suspect that bullheads have the poorest eyesight of the lot, so it would make sense that the flash made by the spinner or perhaps the vibration it makes in the water allows the bullhead to more effectively zero in on its perceived prey.

Who says bullheads won't hit a fly?

Since I've converted 100 percent to fly-fishing, I can honestly say in looking at my fish journals that in the

Oklahoma ponds and lakes I fish, the number of big catfish I've landed just about equal the number of big bass. I never would have dreamed that could be possible based on my early fishing experiences with conventional gear using traditional bass lures and having never caught a catfish of any kind that way. My personal nonscientific theory is that catfish may be more like trout than bass, since they seem to prefer feathers, hair, and fur over plastic, wood, and metal. And here's a final personal opinion on the subject. Just like carp, catfish should be more respected as game fish and need to move up on the snootiness scale within the fly-fishing community. That's why both species have a chapter in this book dedicated exclusively to its kind.

CHAPTER 14

MICROFISHING

've always been a sucker for new and unique fishing challenges. It may have started when, as a boy, I was fishing with my cousin Frank in my Dad's farm pond on a hot summer afternoon and we weren't having any luck. Then, just by complete accident, I twitched my Hula Popper a little bit too close to a huge bullfrog, and *bam!* He nailed it with all the aggressiveness of a lunker largemouth bass. What a total shock that was. What was equally surprising was the fight he gave me by using his long, powerful legs to provide enough resistance to easily bend my limp solid glass rod to a near U-shape. This was back before all those pesky protected cattle egrets migrated to Oklahoma and every pond had a healthy population of bullfrogs in it. Why the law protects these nuisances so they can obliterate our bullfrog population is beyond me, but that's another chapter for another book yet to be written. Anyway, back to my story. Cousin Frank immediately followed suit and tied on a Hula Popper as well, and together we brought home a stringer full of tasty frog legs that my Mom fried for supper that evening. Since then, I've caught snakes, turtles, clams, crabs, and even an angry pelican on a rod and reel, and while they were all freakish incidents, they still provided a sense of curious joy and excitement from being able to attract something with my artificial bait that wasn't a fish.

A fairly recent angling phenomenon that is quickly achieving cult status in this country, and something that has really aroused my curiosity of late, is microfishing. The goal among microanglers is to catch the smallest fish possible. What a strange twist to the traditional longstanding goal of seeking large fish that might be worthy of a man cave mount. It appears to have originated in Japan, where they call it tenago fishing, named after a Japanese native fish that can measure about an inch in length as a full-size adult. Catching a tenago in Japan carries the status and prestige of catching a permit on a fly-rod in the United States and requires an incredible amount of patience and skill. After reading some interesting stories provided on Christopher Stewart's website www.tenkarabum.com, I was intrigued by the notion of going small versus going large in my angling pursuits. But to be honest, I was very skeptical at first. How could I catch a fish two inches or smaller on a hook? What type of bait or artificial fly would I use? Were they even predators that would take a pattern designed to imitate their natural prey? These were mostly minnows, for crying out loud! But after doing my research, I found out that minnows constitute only a small portion of the species available to the microangler and that the vast array of fish available include shiners, chubs, darters, sculpins, mosquitofish, and madtoms, as well as the baby fish of the more traditional gamefish, such as bass, trout, and sunfish. And most of these fish are aggressive predators that can be caught on an artificial lure, if one is smart enough to figure out how to do it. I then did some additional research to see what kind of microfish were available locally and found literally hundreds of species that I had no idea even existed in Oklahoma but freely roamed the local waters all around me. Well, that was all I needed as an incentive—a new challenge. This was something I had to try.

I purchased a 5'10" tenkara rig that I thought would be the most practical way to fish for these diminutive darlings and began to scout out some small local creeks to see what might be in them. The first fishery that looked interesting was a stretch of Coffee Creek that ran close to Arcadia, Oklahoma, off old Route 66, the nation's mother road. It was pretty easy to access from the highway and was only a short walk from where I could park my truck. I had no idea what I'd find or whether my presentation would be the one needed to catch whatever was out there. The smallest fly I had was a size 20 red zebra midge, and even at that size I didn't know whether it would be small enough for the tiny mouths of whatever I was after. When I got to Coffee Creek, I noticed it was crystal clear and running (a rarity in this part of Oklahoma), and had the familiar babbling brook sound that one might hear somewhere in the Rockies. So having the feel of being in the mountains was already exciting and well worth the trip, even if I didn't catch any fish.

The stream wasn't very wide, and I could step across it in many places. I could see a large school of some kind of fish swimming in a little pool, so I tied on the zebra and gave it a shot. On the very first cast, I caught one of the most beautiful fish I'd ever seen anywhere. The body was a bright neon blue, and its fins were florescent orange. I discovered later in doing some research in a reference book I have, *Fishes of Oklahoma*, that it was a red shiner in spawning colors. It's little wonder that today's modern crankbaits can often be found in the same blue-and-orange color combinations. I caught several more later, all no bigger than three inches, and all of them looked like those beautiful tropical fish you see in aquariums in doctor's offices. It's hard to explain my level of excitement, but it was akin to what I had felt when catching my first largemouth bass. I couldn't wait to tell my son Jim and Cousin A. B. about what I had done. Several weeks later, both Jim and A.B. came with me to the same creek, and they had similar success.

A beautiful red shiner caught on a #20 red
Zebra Midge in Coffee Creek.

My next goal was to catch a species that I was very familiar with but was even smaller, a mosquitofish. These little guys can be found in nearly every creek in the state and are live-bearers, just like sharks! I became very familiar with them growing up as a boy and finding them in the small creek that ran through my parents' farm. I would take a minnow trap, bait it with bread, and catch them for bait that I would use for bass and crappie fishing. They rarely approached two inches in size, and most were in the one-inch range. Because they were live-bearers, I used to put them in our stock tank, where they would reproduce every month, and before I knew it, I had my own perpetual supply of live bait whenever I wanted to fish. It was my own personal fish hatchery! The cattle didn't seem to mind having them in their drinking water, but I'm sure a few of them got sucked up occasionally by a thirsty cow.

The question now became, *Could I catch something that small on a fly?* Mosquitofish got their name because they are known for preying on mosquito larvae and thus are used many times as an environmentally safe way to control mosquitos. But their mouths are so small when compared to those of red shiners that I knew I'd have to find a smaller fly than the size I had been successfully using for shiners. When I told A. B. about my next challenge, he told me that Christopher Stewart (a.k.a. Tenkara Bum) had some hooks specially designed for smaller mouths, called tenago hooks, that he imported from Japan for sale in the United States. I got on the website and immediately placed an order. When they arrived in the mail, I estimated their size somewhere in the #30 to #32 range. They were snelled and had an extra short point designed for extremely small mouths like that of the mosquitofish. The string used in the snelled design looked as if it was made of black cotton sewing thread and was obviously a lesser pound test than the 7X tippet I was using on my micro tenkara rig, so I had to take great care in securing the knot to the snelled hook to keep it from breaking off. With a great deal of time and care, I tied two String Thing patterns using tenago hooks, one with white thread and one with red thread, leaving a small piece of thread on both ends to flop around, hoping it might imitate a larva of some kind.

I found a bush to hide behind and, using the white

pattern I had just tied, made my first cast to a group of visible mosquitofish. They all pounced on it like a bunch of piranhas would a piece of raw meat. I mean, these guys were aggressive beyond belief. But actually hooking one was another story. Time after time, I would get one hooked briefly but, as I attempted to bring it out of the water, it would slip off. It may have been that none of them were ever really hooked but just didn't let go of my tiny fly until I lifted them from the water. Finally, a huge 1¾-inch pregnant female managed to get the hook in her mouth, and I finally had her in my hand for a close-up picture with my smartphone before I released her. Here again, my excitement was off the charts for a fish that at one time I had incubated in a stock tank as boy for crappie bait.

A 1¾" western mosquitofish caught on a #32 white String Thing tied on a snelled tenago hook. My most prized microfish to date!

Microfishing also can include pursuing baby fish of larger species, such as trout, sunfish, and catfish. In addition to my small tenkara rigs, I've added a micro fly rod to my microfishing arsenal, and under certain conditions, it is perfect for catching these small guys. The one I have is made from a five-foot Rainshadow blank and matched with a miniscule two-inch diameter reel loaded with DT1F line. I love using it on the Rio Hondo in New Mexico, where there always seems to be an abundance of willing rainbows and browns four inches and under, with dry flies size 20 or smaller being at the top of their menu. Another small stream where my son Jim and I had good success catching baby trout was West Tensleep Creek in Wyoming. My nephew, Dolph Prater, took us there on a trip we made to his home in Casper, Wyoming, and like the Hondo, it was full of microfish who seemed to crave dry flies. Jim even caught a rare baby tiger trout (a brown-and-brook hybrid) on that fishery using his tenkara rig.

A rare tiger trout caught on a Stimulator by my son Jim on West Tensleep Creek in the Bighorn National Forest in Wyoming.

In pursuing baby fish in Oklahoma lakes and ponds, I will look for riprap and clusters of rocks that provide hiding places from predators for small fish. When I've located the perfect-looking rock structure, I'll dap a #20 nymph pattern into a crevice and watch a longear or green sunfish dart out from the shadows to nab what he thinks is an easy meal. It's so much fun to watch them come from out of nowhere with lightning quickness. The antics of these little fish remind me of a jack-in-the-box toy. You never know when the clown is emerging, but you know it will sometime, and it still surprises you. Sometimes you'll hook into something much larger by accident using this method, such as a nine-inch bluegill, and then you have a real battle on your hands with a rig that wasn't intended to handle a fish that large.

This baby green sunfish darted out from his hiding place in the riprap to nab a #22 olive String Thing. Ounce for ounce, these little greenies will give you as much fight as any gamefish in the lake.

It has also happened to me with trout. One time I was microfishing with my tenkara rig for some unidentified baitfish that appeared to be feeding aggressively off the rocks in about a foot of water in Roaring River. I put on a size 22 white String Thing and begin dapping at the cluster of fish just about three feet from shore. They never showed any interest in my fly, but from out of nowhere a ten-inch rainbow charged out from the deep to nail my tiny fly, and then I had a battle that was nip and tuck for an extended period of time before I eventually landed her. To this day, I have no idea where she came from or how she was able to see a fly that small from so far away.

A similar thing happened to me with a nine-inch wild brown trout on the Rio Hondo, and I literally had to get into the stream and follow the fish up and down the river to keep from breaking off. Remember: you have no reel on a tenkara rig, so following her with my rod was the only option I had to keep from breaking off my 7X tippet. I felt like someone in the suburbs walking an oversize Great Dane who wants to go faster than its owner is willing to walk and holding on the leash for dear life. I'm glad nobody saw me splashing up and down that little shallow stream, high-sticking my little 5' 10" rod until I was able to finally wear her out! It just proves that those shallow little streams can sometimes produce some unexpected larger fish.

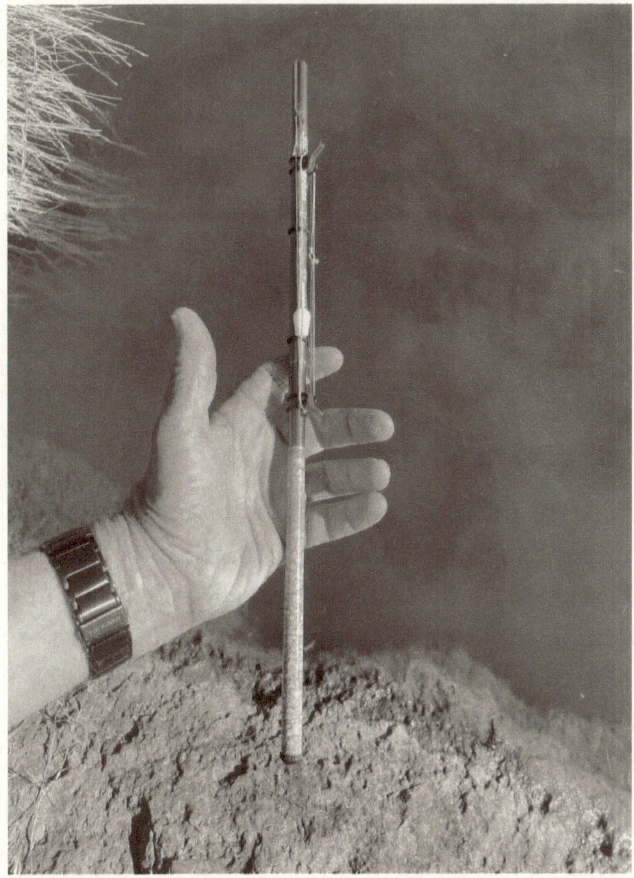

My preferred rig for microfishing: a tenkara rod that
measures only fifteen inches but telescopes to nearly
six feet. This one is ready to go fishing, complete with
a strike indicator, 7X tippet, and a #22 nymph.

It's hard to explain why I can get so excited about catching
little bitty fish, but I think Matthew L. Miller said it best in
an article he wrote for *Field & Stream* when he theorized,
"The concentration required in tempting a small fish to bite
is as close to meditation as I'm likely to get." I would certainly
concur with that statement, and if that type of fanaticism
might be described by some as a cult, then I'm a follower!

CHAPTER 15

TENKARA

Similar to microfishing, tenkara is another recent trend among fishermen that is approaching cult status. Like Western style fly-fishing, Eastern style fly-fishing, as it is sometimes referred to, requires that you cross the ocean to be able to trace its roots. Only in this case, it's the Pacific rather than the Atlantic ocean. Tenkara, which originated in the high mountain regions of Japan's main island, employs a rig that has no fly line, no backing, no reel, and no rings on the rod. The rod is telescoping and most commonly ranges in length from ten to fifteen feet. Attached to the end of the rod is a short piece of braid called a lillian. Attached to the lillian is a leader about the same length of the rod. During the presentation of the fly, the line can be fished totally out of the water, as the rod is held high so that the rod and the line form a ninety-degree angle. This provides some obvious advantages to the fly-fisher. With no line in the water, there's much less opportunity to spook the fish, and strike sets are much more reliable because slack line is a thing of the past, as is mending—what an advantage this creates for drifting nymphs and dry flies!

With the absence of slack line, hook-up percentages increase substantially. While I've never kept actual track, I would estimate that with a fly rod and reel, my personal successful dry fly hook-up percentage, on a good day, ranges between 15 and 20 percent. Dead drifting a nymph, even with a strike indicator, isn't much better. But just for fun, and after back-to-back success with hook-ups the first time I used a tenkara rod with my favorite dry fly, I began keeping track to see how many consecutive fish I could land relative to takes, similar to the way a basketball player might keep track of how many consecutive free throws he or she can make. I broke my streak at fifteen consecutive fish. That, for me, was phenomenal. Streamers can also be successfully fished with a tenkara rig by simply leading the fly with the rod. Early fly-fishermen all over the world used some form of fixed line method to present flies to catch fish. In Japan, fly-fishers went from cane poles to jointed cane poles and eventually to telescoping rods using modern materials. The evolution of fly-fishing in Western cultures took a somewhat different path by adding reels with sophisticated fly lines.

Tenkara is ideal for microfishing, which really was the genesis for its development many years ago. The mountain streams in Japan typically flow over beds of volcanic rock and sediment that are steep, turbulent, and fast moving. Compared to the nutrient-rich rivers and streams found in Europe, these streams are ecologically poor. As a result, trout and char species inhabiting them do not have the luxury of abundant food sources and consequently are much smaller. Rigs designed to catch these small fish have to be small and efficient, and these types of rigs fit the bill perfectly. I love using a six-foot rod with a 7X tippet for microfish, which I suspect may have been the rig of choice for those early tenkara pioneers of seventeenth-century Japan. With the currently available carbon fiber technology, today tenkara is not confined to small fish, and rigs can be found on the market these days designed for catching much larger fish—trophies that any fly-fisher would be proud to hang on his or her wall. And as this chapter is written, tenkara purists all over the world are pushing the envelope and having success landing bigger and bigger fish both in freshwater and saltwater with no end in sight.

My own personal experience with tenkara started out very shaky. Cousin A. B. is a dyed-in-the wool tenkara fanatic and has had great success. He seemed to always have so much fun with Eastern style fly-fishing that I had to try it myself. I'll never forget the first fish I hooked on a tenkara rig—a fourteen-inch rainbow on Roaring River in the Missouri Ozarks. A. B. happened to be standing nearby, and this being my first tenkara fish, I was so excited not only to get a solid hook-up but also to do it in front of him. But I quickly learned that playing a fish and landing it on a tenkara outfit requires a completely different skill set than those I had developed in learning how to fly-fish Western style.

Let's see now, I had a twelve-foot rod attached to twelve feet of line with no way to reel the fish in! Simple math told me the fish was approximately twenty-four feet away from me, and as far as I could tell, it would stay that way forever, because I couldn't, for the life of me, figure out a way to bring it in to shore—or, for that matter, within reach of my landing net. After thoroughly playing her out, and with too much personal pride to ask A. B. what to do next, I simply faked it for a while and pretended to simply enjoy the fight she was putting up as if I knew exactly what I was doing. With the unfortunate fish almost dead from exhaustion, I finally put my rod on the ground and grabbed the line and started pulling it toward me hand over hand. I was hoping that nobody would see what I was doing, but I'm sure someone did. I felt just like I did when I was nine years old and caught my first big catfish in Uncle Chuck's pond and, upon feeling more resistance than I was prepared for, just put the rod over my shoulder and began walking away from the water with the fish in tow. Of course, that wasn't all that embarrassing, because I was only nine, for crying out loud, and nobody expected much. But now I was a grown adult and was hoping to show a little more dignity than I displayed that day in landing my first fish using a tenkara rig.

I'd like to tell you that since that somewhat embarrassing day, I've mastered tenkara, but I'd be lying if I did. At least now I've gotten a little more sophisticated in my landing techniques and have managed to land trout, bass, catfish, and crappie as big as two pounds. While it's still pretty nerve-racking not having the advantage of a reel equipped with a sophisticated drag, I learned from A. B. that keeping a steady pressure with the rod straight up over the fish makes it less likely for it to make a long run, which of course would be a disaster with no way to yield line. The significantly longer length of the rod allows you to maintain constant vertical pressure while playing the fish rather than the horizontal pressure it may be used to. It seems like the fish is a little confused by the feeling of vertical line pressure as opposed to horizontal line pressure and just sort of fights in place. At least, that's my theory. Maybe that's why the Japanese refer to this type of fishing as tenkara, which, loosely translated into English, means, "from the top." Another technique I learned from A. B. is to try to lead the fish into multiple slow figure-eight patterns during the fight in an effort to increase its fatigue to the point it can be netted.

And while we're talking about A. B., I should mention that it's a supreme joy just to watch him using his tenkara rig. He's a master at it, and the way he works the rod is truly poetry in motion. He may have obtained that gift naturally because of good genetics. His mother, my aunt Lillian, who was always called Aunt Lil by her nieces and nephews, loved to fish and excelled at catching big bass using a long cane pole attached to a few feet of braided line with minnows and a bobber. Did I just describe tenkara fishing with a strike indicator? While the rest of us were catching small sunfish and stunted crappie with our spinning rigs, she was catching quality-sized bass with her cane pole. Even A. B. couldn't figure out how his mom always managed to outfish us, but she had all of us in envy mode with her ability to coax bass into a feeding frenzy.

Even though Aunt Lil wasn't aware of it at the time, we now know she was using tenkara-type techniques with her cane pole. I remember whenever she found out I was getting ready to go fishing, she would always say to me, "Tommy, be sure and catch Old Joe for me. He's a smart one, but someday one of us is going to catch him." I'm not sure just how big "Old Joe" was, but that mythical image of something very large and nasty down in the depths of whatever pond or lake I was fishing always served as motivation for me, at a very young age, to be the eternal optimist and always expect to catch something really big. Just like the giant marlin that Santiago finally caught in Ernest Hemingway's novel *The Old Man and the Sea*, I'm never going to give up trying to land Aunt Lil's "Old Joe."

CHAPTER 16

I HEAR YOU KNOCKIN'

Several years ago, on a fishing trip to New Mexico, I stepped in a deep hole and fell during a hike to one of my favorite fishing spots on the Rio Grande. X-rays revealed that I had broken a bone in my right leg. For the next four months, I was in a walking boot cast. As a result of doing some lopsided walking with a boot on one foot and a street shoe on the other, I noticed that a mild case of occasional sciatica that I previously had turned more severe and progressively got worse over time. To deal with the ongoing discomfort, I've seen a chiropractor, worn a back brace, gone through physical therapy, tried Rolfing, Pilates, radiofrequency, muscle relaxers, pain patches, and medication of all types, including CBD, but nothing seems to work—nothing, that is, except for having a fish on the end of my line!

Now that I'm retired and have more time to spend on the water, I'll look outside and see what a beautiful day it is and think to myself, *What a perfect day to fish.* I'll start getting all my gear to together and start feeling that sharp pain that goes all the way down my right leg and think, *How bad do I really want to do this?* The thought of loading up my heavy Hobie Cat kick boat into the truck or standing for long periods of time casting a fly rod just seems to be too tiring to justify the anticipated pain. But then I'll reflect on what else I've got planned for the day, which is basically nothing. And isn't this what I've always worked hard for—a chance to go fishing whenever I want and wherever I want? I also think of all the guilt I would have at the end of the day, lying on my comfortable couch in the man cave watching TV reruns with all those countless ads on Medicare supplement plans, walk-in tubs, and stand-up walkers. How depressing is that? I'm not going to let a little bit of pain blow this for me at this stage of my life. And besides, if the fishing is good and my pole gets bent, something magical always seems to happen. The pain just goes away. It's temporary, but it's real. The problem, of course, is what if I don't catch any fish? It used to be that just getting out enjoying the scenery and the challenge of getting a take was all I needed. It still is, but now it's accompanied with some physical pain that just won't go away until I have a fish on the end of my line. Never in my twenties did I ever imagine that my beloved sport would turn out to also be physically therapeutic. It's always been therapeutic mentally, but this is a new twist.

So what I do in my seventies is just force myself out the door, grimace through the pain, and get after it. It's kind of like the song recently written by country and western singer-song writer and fellow Oklahoman Toby Keith, who was inspired by a conversation he had on a golf course with Clint Eastwood. Mr. Eastwood was getting ready to celebrate his eighty-eighth birthday, and Toby asked him how he was going to celebrate it. Eastwood replied, "I'm going to begin work on my new movie, *The Mule.*" Impressed by his boundless energy at an age when many would be content to just sit on the front porch and watch the cars go by, Toby asked Clint how he keeps going. He responded, "I just get up every morning and go out and don't let the old man in." Keith was inspired by that response and wrote a song titled "Don't Let the Old Man In."

As a fisherman firmly entrenched in the aging baby boomer generation, that song has served as a battle hymn for me as the aches and pains have seemed to mount with every approaching birthday. My family physician just smiles and says it's normal and that I have birthday disease. "You keep having those birthdays," he says, "and you're going to eventually start having all those aches and pains." Great! Just what everyone needs—a family doctor who thinks he's a comedian! But he's a wonderful person and a very competent doctor, and I wouldn't want anyone else to be my primary health-care practitioner.

Lest I allow the final chapter (pun intended) of this book to get too dark, let me clarify that I share Clint Eastwood's philosophy only to make a point. I'm hopeful we're all going to have enough birthdays to get old, and it's how we get there that makes the difference between being a happy member of the geriatric tribe or a resentful, bitter one. Pain can come at any age and for any number of reasons, and it would be a terrible shame if we let it get in the way of doing what really makes us happy. Find that special something that makes you happy and just do it, even if it means putting up with some physical discomfort. For me it's fly-fishing. And the best way I've found to continue doing what makes me happy is to never let the old man in to prevent me from fishing. In reflecting on all this, another hit tune comes to mind. It's the old Fats Domino rock 'n' roll hit of the sixties that begins with the lyrics, "I hear you knocking, but you can't come in." I don't know how that old man found my house in Edmond, Oklahoma, but he did, and when he comes knocking, I can assure you he ain't getting in for a long, long time as long as there are fish out there that still haven't been caught.

BIBLIOGRAPHY

Applefeld, Cathy Olson. "Toby Keith Explains How Clint Eastwood Inspired Don't Let The Old Man In for The Mule." Billboard. December 15, 2018. www.billboard.com.

Davenport, John H. *Get Into Fly-fishing - For Under $100.* Denver, CO: John Davenport, 2014.

Duda, Steve. "My Bad." *The Flyfish Journal* 9, no 2.

Ellis, Jack. *Bassin' with a Fly Rod.* North Conway, NH: Mountain Pond Publishing, 1994.

Gierach, John. *Sex, Death, and Fly-Fishing.* New York: Simon & Schuster/Fireside, 1990.

Gierach, John. *Standing in a River Waving a Stick.* New York: Simon & Schuster/Fireside, 1999.

Hemingway, Ernest. *The Old Man And The Sea.* New York: Charles Scribner's Sons, 1952.

Lucas, Jason. *Lucas on Bass Fishing.* New York: Dodd, Mead & Company, 1962.

Maclean, Norman. *A River Runs Through It and Other Stories.* Chicago: The University of Chicago Press, 2001.

Miller, Matthew L. *Fishing Through the Apocalypse: An Angler's Adventures in the 21st Century.* Lanham, MD: Lyons Press, 2019.

Miller, Rudolph J., and Henry W. Robinson. *Fishes Of Oklahoma.* Norman, OK: University of Oklahoma Press, 2004.

Reynolds, Barry, Brad Befus, and John Berryman. *Carp on the Fly: A Flyfishing Guide.* Boulder, CO: Johnson Books, 1997.

Steward, Dick, and Farrow Allen. *Flies for Bass & Panfish.* Intervale, NH: Northland Press, Inc. 1992.

Whitelaw, Ian. *The History of Fly-Fishing in Fifty Flies.* New York: Stewart, Tabori & Chang, 2015.